I M A

GINE

I B

EEN

DOUGLAS KEARNEY

SCIE

N C E

FIC

TION

A L W

WAVE BOOKS

AYS

SEATTLE / NEW YORK

Published by Wave Books

www.wavepoetry.com

Wave Books titles are distributed to the trade by

Consortium Book Sales and Distribution

Phone: 800-283-3572 / SAN 631-760X

Library of Congress Cataloging-in-Publication Data

Names: Kearney, Douglas, author.

Title: I imagine I been science fiction always / Douglas Kearney.

Description: Seattle, WA : Wave Books, 2025.

Identifiers: LCCN 2024038701 | ISBN 9798891060128 (paperback)

Subjects: LCGFT: Visual poetry.

Classification: LCC PS3611.E177 I2 2025 | DDC 811/.6—dc23/eng/20240828

LC record available at https://lccn.loc.gov/2024038701

Designed by Crisis

Printed in Canada

9 8 7 6 5 4 3 2 1

First Edition

Wave Books 121

FOR MARCIA KEARNEY,

NICOLE MCJAMERSON,

YONA HARVEY,

PAM NOLES,

MACKITY SMACK,

LAUREN HALSEY,

TRUGOY THE DOVE,

CHRIS HARRISON,

& GREG TATE

I IMAGINE I BEEN SCIENCE FICTION ALWAYS

/

SHUTTLEBLACK GETTIN UP EPIC

/

OVER DELUXE AF

/

DARK MATTER ARMORY FLEX

/

THAT LOUD-ASSED COLORED SILENCE: TURNTABLISM

/

SHADOW, YO(U)

ACKNOWLEDGMENTS

I just wanted to write some fly shit.

—LaTasha N. Nevada Diggs

I IMAGINE I BEEN

SCIENCE FICTION ALWAYS

AFTER TEO RIVERA-DUNDAS

C F G I I.

A AA

B C EE E I I

C E

E

.II L M N N

I N O

N

S S T W Y

I been queried *in re*
my "nature" then answered
"Why: I'm opposite to";
an objectionable
object whipped up as such.

To uselessness — I was,
to wit — instrumental.
To be played [out] — *n.b.*
[SEE] a pianola —
e.g. I play myself —
ha! Vis: *vernacular* —
ha ha! Vis: *literal* —
ha ha ha! It's complex,
but this ITness needful.

Figure me a simple machine? I'd flex some pull, have leverage, could screw with their jive THEIRness, yes? Lay plain their intention.

But *complex* what one call
“equivocation.” Smoke
that’s lexical. *Complex*:
as in “got me a *complex*
off of my nature as
fixed opposite.” *Complex*:
Prison industrial.
But is their need to need
some opposite nature
to be being *complex*?
One could work janky shit
up in that word: *complex*.

They pass off that shit as natural shit. Which shit? *Their* shit. *Their* shit need *my* nature opposite.

Opposite to what? *Yes,* dear Interlocutor!

Swear I *ain't* natural
by *their* uncanny shit:
— that supernatural?
— forged as both object *and*
their jury-rigged figment?

I imagine I been
science fiction always —
even as was *they* done
sailed unidentified
floating obscenities.

To whom that natural?

Sure as shit it's shady
calling all those tall ships
kin, kith; isn't we forged
from the same industry?

[SEE] a pianola — They pass off that shit as Prison too haphazard
Swear I ain't natural

Were I forced to answer
for my nature — call
me batty — but I'd aver
maybe 50/50
odds you'd find some nature
to me. Seems what's in me's
too haphazard for blood.

Its nature's *contingent*.

Which I means to say: it
mess some hands, ain't hardly
ever blood — rather, shit.

Some *register* of shit.

ndustrial. that's lexical. Complex:
complex what one call
ever as was they done

But see it at my feet —
running like it can't wait
to break north from out me —
right then, right there, it's blood.

Thus, I don't guess that shit
they spot me with is flesh
yet it sure isn't not.

[SEE] a pianola —Swear I ain't natural Prison too haphazard
machine? I'd flex some pull, They pass off that shit as
ha ha ha!
Never blood -— rather, shit. by th

an Figure IT objec me
ne opposite nature

ria: bloo

I imagine I been
science fiction always —
I imagine I been
science fiction always —
I imagine I been
science fiction always —
I imagine I been
science fiction always —
I imagine I been
science fiction always —
I imagine I been
science fiction always —
I imagine I been
science fiction always —
I imagine I been
science fiction always —

industrial. that's lexical. Complex:
complex what one call
even as was they done
It's complex, plain
canny shit: Lay mess P some their hands ain't hardly intention.
X odds you'd find some nature
simple
onable a Were I forced to ar
Sure as shit it's shady

What my but to guess a

a! For an word Which equivocation. Smiled she:

sure ain't off la natural they — to flesh force science

hen one plain their kith; — 50/50 complex

as ha to,

I

I imagine I been

I science fiction always —

I imagine I been

science fiction always — fiction

science fiction always —

I imagine I been

imagine imagine I been fiction

science fiction always —

science fiction always —

imagine I imagine I been

science fiction always always

fiction always

I imagine imagine always been

I science fiction always —

science imagine I been

I science fiction always —

science fiction always —

science fiction always —

IT

jury-rigged figment? I been

play myself —

always

Swear I ain't natural Prison

[SEE] a pianola — too haphazard

machine? I'd flex some pull'

They pass off that shit as by th

Never an ha ha objec

some blood — rather, shit. me a

Figure

opposite

natur they spot me w

[SEE] right

a ra! bloo
shit e- pull, uselessness shit g-
Have me' done my it's north
in't leverage, kin,

I
I
I fiction imagine I been I
always been
I science fiction always —
I imagine
I imagine I been science
fiction
always science fiction fiction
science always —
imagine been
I
imagine always imagine been been
science I
science fiction always been fiction
imagine fiction been
I imagine been
science fiction always always
fiction always
imagine
imagine I been
fiction
always fiction
science imagine been always
science fiction always —
I science fiction I been
been
science always fiction
always
I been
I
always
always
—
fiction
I I always
—
industrial. I Complex:
imagine
lexical.
that's even as was they done
Lay plain their intention.
ncanny shit:
It's complex what one call
onable complex,
mess some hands, ain't hardly
simple Sure as shit it's shady
X odds you'd find some na
Were I forced
is flesh to a

opposite from e.g. all Smoke been hazard m
Vis: call batty need tallships — In
there ha! It to off shit Vis: I'm ure be ain
to to Lay ,, what's
That my but to guess a
a! For an word: Which equivocation. Sailed shit:
ha to , a ha
sure ain't off the — to flesh forcette scie
shit.— both too it's that shit
identified shady
What they natu
—50/50 complex
imagine As was, object nature
flex could play complex figment
played sure that's I
been
always science from indu
some aver jive some
fiction
II I
I fiction fiction
always
imagine fiction been been
I been
object "nature" my fiction always science
I imagine
I
always sI — I been
jury-rigged never Com
fiction ha
fiction science I been ple
always ample yea? Comp
fiction
pianola — Prison
machine? [SEE] a Swear I ain't natural too haphazard
I'd flex some pull, They pass off that shit as
site
by the
blood
Never an — rather, ha shit. ha object
with
odds Figure they
maybe spot me
me spot opposite nature tal [SEE] me

ne by—or as even—supernatur-
answer and not. al? you'd I
feet I always wit
off The flesh be
I bless are of hands, ha
blood
shit "e- full, useless ess shit Fig-
la natural I'd they
It's nature yet can't nat- ture being some oppo-
been
piano- imagine
Pass as out it
Seems but what? their They "got
I
—at I could whom there is- imagine
been
I un canny imagine [out] been spot maybe odds with
always I I
fiction II I fiction
ed science imagine been
imagine
I I I I I science
I science
I
always
my in—I needful. in
always science fiction science
fiction
I been
IT always I I
ne always
fiction
ustrial imagine
that's lexical. always Complex:
even as was they done
we shit regi- Lay plain their intention.
canny shit:
complex what one call
science
onable
it's comes complex, some hands, ain't hardly X
Were a I forced to answer
simple
n
is flesh
Sure as shit it's shady

to to Lay smoke work up forge are aint ha' nature
vis: call need tallships in been
From e.g. all ha! It to off shit. Vis:
identified shady my opposite batty what's there, I'm hazard n
ha! For an word: but could to guess
Which equivocation" fated shit.
That sure ain't off the — flesh be sci
as ha to a
shit — both too it's that shit nature
plex THEIRness, their those What they
imagine 50/50 figment
flex As was, object nature
I been I
nable played sure that's Play from after IT ural with runni in
fiction instru- com-
n.b. ha need Oppo plex
I I I Some live
fiction always fiction some
I I been
imagine science
shit. Me fiction instru-
object "nature" my h
Were I I Figure a
always locutor! Answered com-
fiction jury-rigged Com pl
isn't swear I science
Complex, to
this I been answer simple yes? Com
machine? always fiction
forced me Prison in
"Why: to piano la
[SEE] a Swear I ain't natural too haphazard
I'd flex then, They pass off that shit as
a some pull, Is find One floating
see literal a
-do Their To
object n o
hardly ha
Never ha — rather, they spot ha
some
odds opposite shit.
maybe with nature me
posite." Their that Inter- Were I
[SEE]
en spot al? call right myself mac

icel it I I shit. But calling

answer and not. ITness as always of

the by—of as fear be wit even—supernatu

al? you'd I dear to

uselessness shit Fig-

no- shit blood pull

a! Prison re same shit? I'd they

agent. ture being some oppo-

nature yet can't nat- imagine Seems but natural been

Pass as out what? their They "got

—a blood.—some Thus, contin it

—at I could whom imagine

there is- been

I I janky blood. To vernac

un- I ular but say: But Sure

always I I I I maybe odds with

fiction I I I been spot fiction

I I been

d science imagine I

intention. me hands, I mental science

nature I

my always I — I

always in— needful. s c i

fiction

science fiction in

x n I been

ne always fiction

odds you'd find

always I — any

some nature

trial. lexical. always Complex:

imagine that's

even as was they done

we shit regi-

y their uncanny shit: their intention. [no] imagine

is Lay plain

complex what one call science

ctionable

It's complex, mess some hands, lol ain't hardly

whipped up queried I mental then, see hardly

flesh site fixed screw rather,—wait

simple

ced answer as—as

to Sure as shit it's shady break ns complex? In means

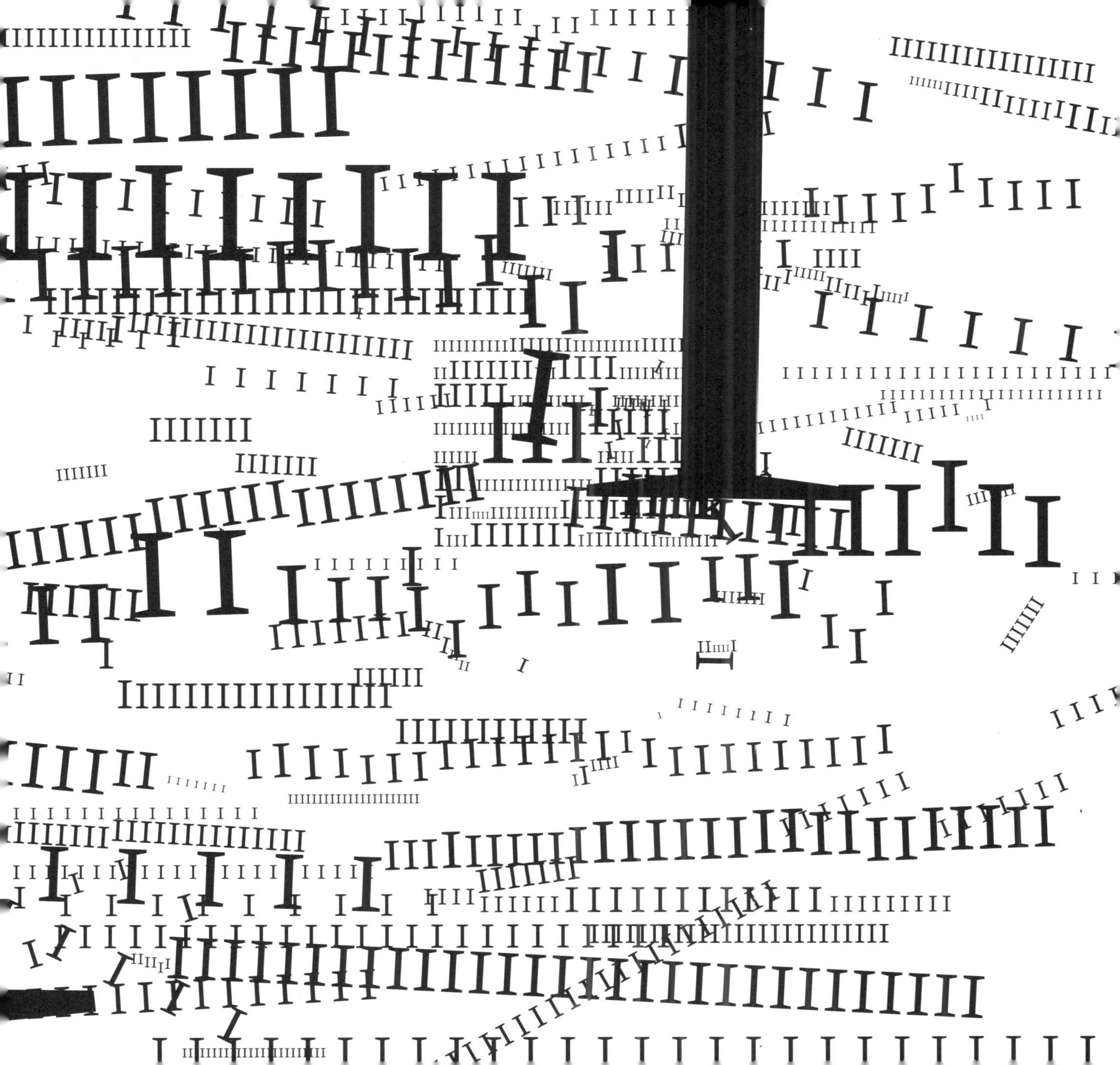

1

alwa
alwa
alwa
alwa
alw

SHUTTLEBLACK

GETTIN UP EPIC

RUN! I'VE GOT TO

RUN! I'VE GOT TO!
I'LL DIE!

CAN'T RUN!
...I'LL DIE FIGHTING

...I'LL DIE

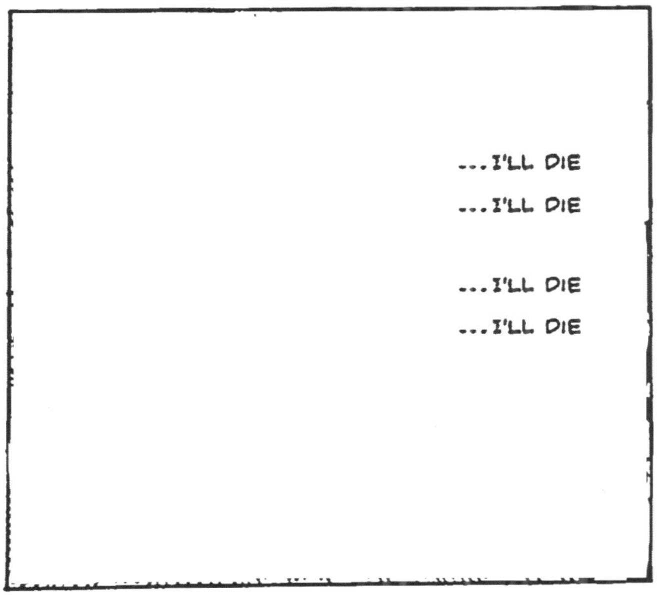
...I'LL DIE
...I'LL DIE
...I'LL DIE
...I'LL DIE

...I'LL DIE

...I'LL DIE

...I'LL

...I'LL

...I'LL DIE

...I'LL DIE

...I'LL DIE

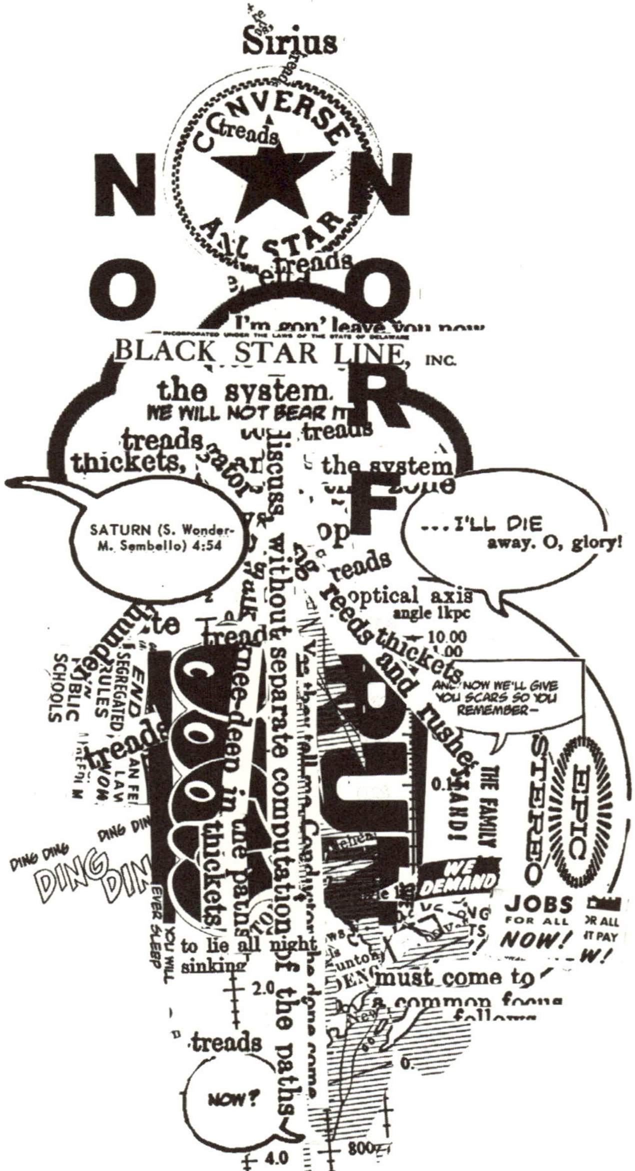

Sirius
CONVERSE
treads
ALL STAR
N
O
N
O
R
F
I'm gon' leave you now
BLACK STAR LINE, INC.
the system
WE WILL NOT BEAR
treads
thickets,
the system
discuss without separate computation of the paths
SATURN (S. Wonder-M. Sembello) 4:54
...I'LL DIE
away. O, glory!
optical axis
angle 1kpc
reeds
thickets
and
rushes
NOW WE'LL GIVE YOU SCARS SO YOU REMEMBER—
knee-deep in the paths
thickets
STEREO
EPIC
THE FAMILY STAND!
WE DEMAND
JOBS FOR ALL NOW!
PUBLIC SCHOOLS
SEGREGATED RULES
END
DING DING
DING DING
DING DING
YOU WILL NEVER SLEEP
to lie all night sinking
must come to
a common focus
treads
NOW?
2.0
4.0
800

NOW?

OVER DELUXE AF

[L+R=1]

What had happened was.

it has been necessary to take freely

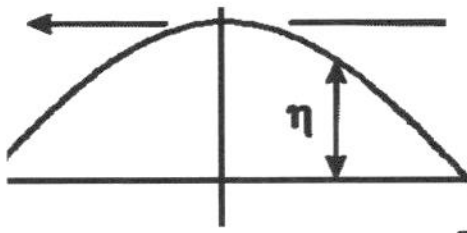

RATE OF CLIMB FROM STANDARD SEA
LEVEL VALUES HERE.

THOUSANDS OF FEET

1st SEMICHOR.

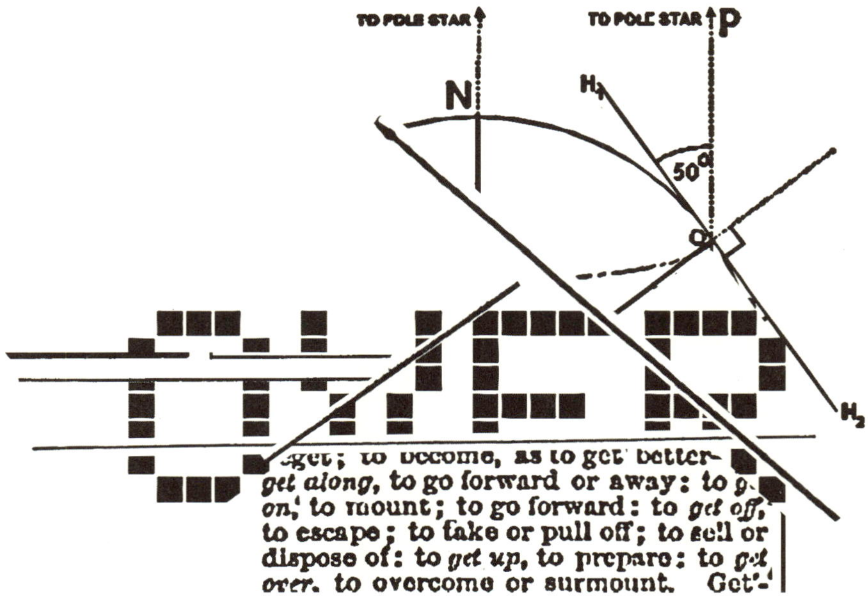
TO POLE STAR
TO POLE STAR
P
N
50°
O
get; to become, as to get better-
get along, to go forward or away: to g
on, to mount; to go forward: to get off,
to escape; to fake or pull off; to sell or
dispose of: to get up, to prepare: to get
over, to overcome or surmount. Get'-

Techne, maybe?
To *over* as in *-come*.
A kind of capital, kind of.
A gain from losses?

When paired with *get* becomes an inheritance
of persistent parabolic visioning.
Wastrels spendthrift it to a *tsk*:
Get over it already!
The "it," appears an obstacle.
Often, say anatomical—blood wet despite
how long ago the cut.
And whodunnit?
Lemme see them hands.

Fun for one's done once no lives left:
i.e. given no quarter

For another fun leaves no life:
e.g. gives no quarter.

Depends which side of the______________you on.

u) gun

s) river

a) definition

"This shouldn't be about sides..."

that's game.

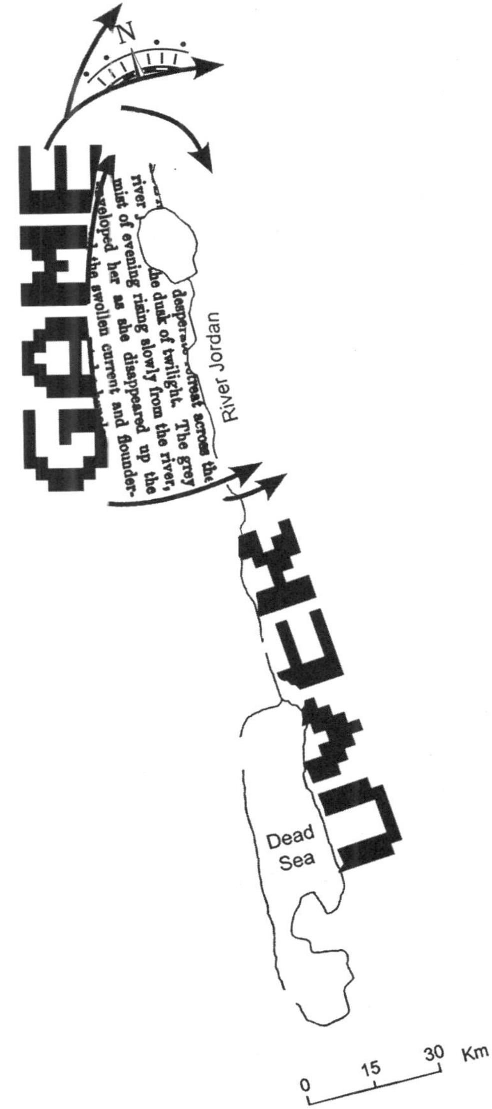
N
River Jordan
Dead
Sea
0
15
30
Km

X
FROM
THE STARS

Hey diddle Doodle.

We's the hole kit and caboodle of the under what bottoms
your bogus top.

We's the doormat of your stoop.

We's the outcasts showing you inside.
We's here to tell you: if you still see stars overhead in there,
maybe what you figured for *spyglass*
is a *nightstick*,
and when you called yourself -*gazing*,
you was being -*struck*.

The transcendence hustle is distinct
from the sublime too high to get too low to get.
Transcendence makes context ghost.
To ghost is to stay despite being gone.
Thus: though one transcends a no-way
the no-way remains, hainting.
Ghost-ass hustle!
Now: to get to a too high or too
low to get to is to live in a where one cannot be.
Black life matter.
Lift ev'ry voice like a rocket.
Turf ev'ry voice like a root.
Hold and hold and hold the note.

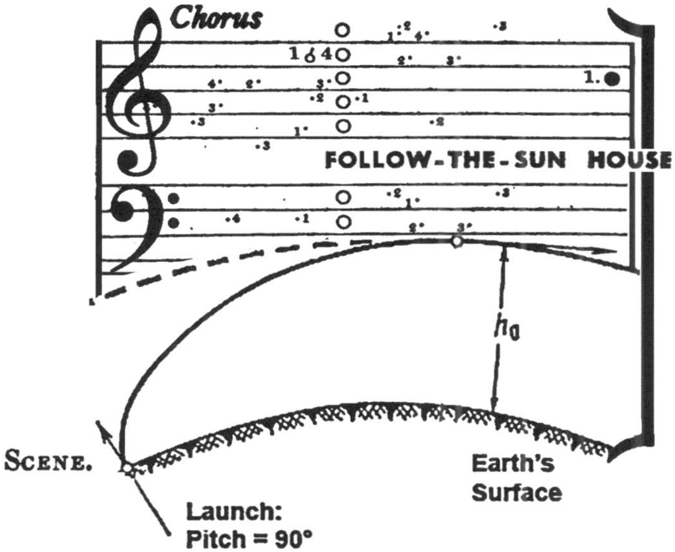

Chorus
FOLLOW-THE-SUN HOUSE
h_0
Scene.
Earth's Surface
Launch:
Pitch = 90°

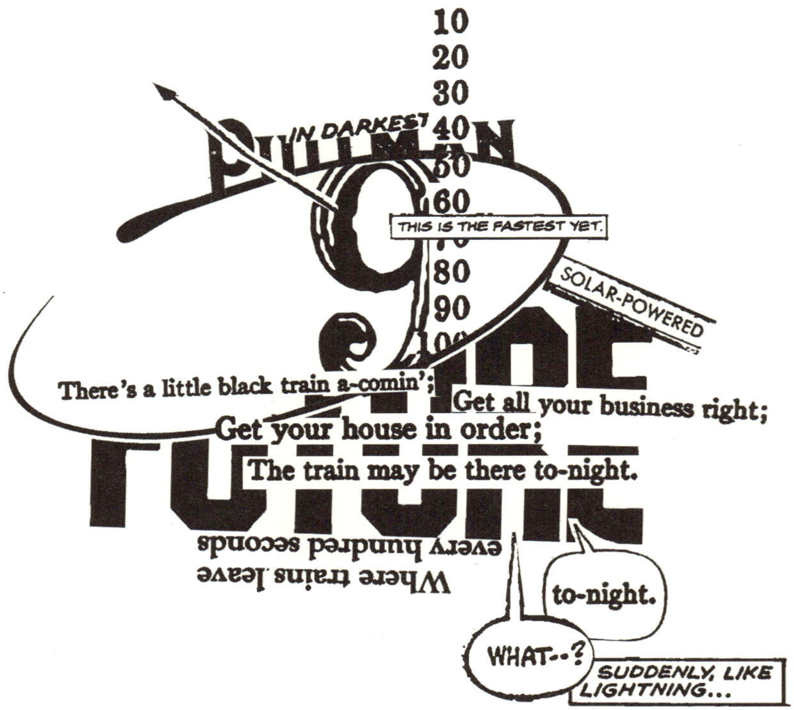
10
20
30
40
50
60
80
90
IN DARKEST
PULLMAN
THIS IS THE FASTEST YET.
SOLAR-POWERED
There's a little black train a-comin';
Get all your business right;
Get your house in order;
The train may be there to-night.
Where trains leave
every hundred seconds
to-night.
WHAT--?
SUDDENLY, LIKE LIGHTNING...

MAGA wants a do over to when their baggage
totes was totes by Others toted as they they they
went on their way.

Their go-back urge a locomotive propelled
assbackwards, the present puked at the future.

One wonders what they fevered to chuck up their
chronic progress jonesing.

In what tunnel?
To what end?
Of what light?

From high his dug planet, Ish is all.
you talk over a and *booming out* —

That's some of that supersonic flight chant.
Up in a theater Black chat shatters atmosphere.
Up, here, is what was once Nigger Heaven hung
up a dark room casting light side-eye.
Downstairs where the pit used to was,
patrons reckon amusement as silence ordinance.
STFU.GTFOH.
The monster's in the basement! wings from
the upper floor as the flickering star's lips
part like chasms to leap.

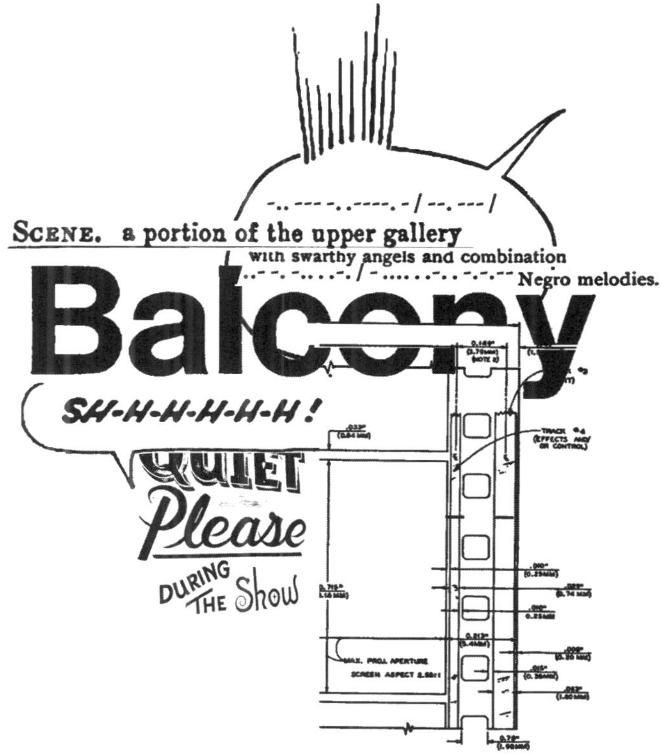
SCENE. a portion of the upper gallery
with swarthy angels and combination
Negro melodies.
Balcony
SH-H-H-H-H-H!
QUIET
Please
DURING THE Show
TRACK #4 (EFFECTS AND/OR CONTROL)
MAX. PROJ. APERTURE
SCREEN ASPECT 2.55:1

SUDDENLY...
THE END
MOMENTS LATER...
la, la, la, la, la, la, la, la, la,
home is o - ver Jor - dan,

Whose was? the first question that November
morn after it was over.

Whose hadn't begun?

To get myself back, I fixed to remember what I cut
to pin me to the all-in-this-together yonder.

Y'all, I saw there a sad so new was still pink
and wailing.

I felt like a Black-ass nipple.

Speculative don't always turn out *fi*.

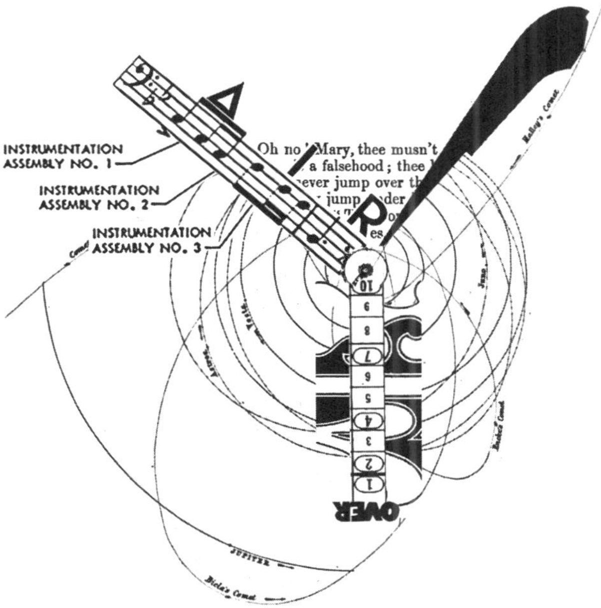

INSTRUMENTATION
ASSEMBLY NO. 1
INSTRUMENTATION
ASSEMBLY NO. 2
INSTRUMENTATION
ASSEMBLY NO. 3
Oh no ' Mary, thee musn't
a falsehood; thee
Halley's Comet
JUPITER
Biela's Comet

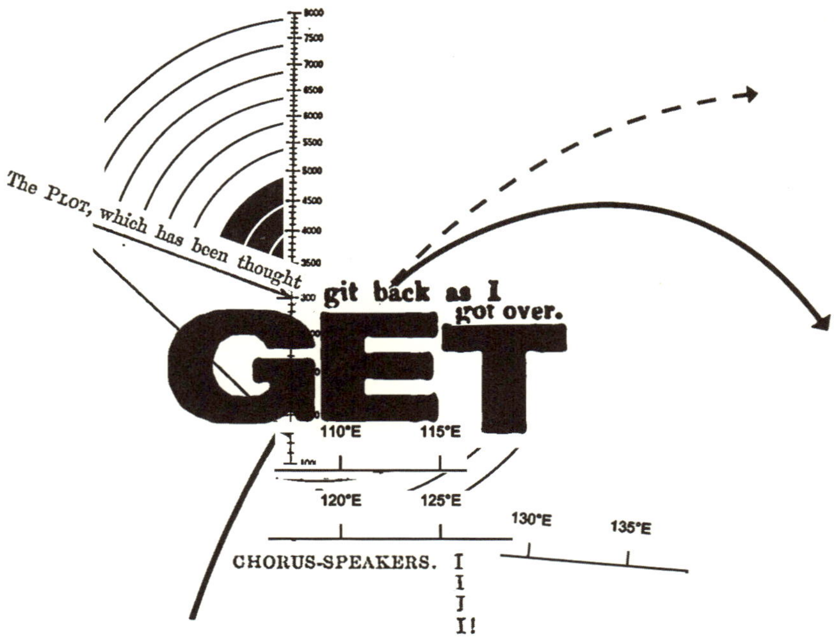

The PLOT, which has been thought
git back as I
got over.
GET
110°E
115°E
120°E
125°E
130°E
135°E
CHORUS-SPEAKERS.
I
I
J
I!

Saturday at the Black wedding, we rocked
"The Big Payback."

Rapped in sync with our late Godfather,
who still still, lay above ground.

Slid we, over the screwface floor.
We got up, goodfooting it right on down.

Emancipation's not its *raison* for raising.
Better I see by C.Smith's[1] lit shade.
I'm calling up Cauleen for to say AfroFuturism
does what it does when how what it does it with
is how it stay doing what it be doing
without only doing what it's done been doing.[2]
Mmmm.

Mashing "Dirty Computer Love" through
Bluestooth,
flying's not always away, but sometimes a ways
over for a cool lick of fresh Black sky.
From up here, I may happen to hear: some dooms
don't favor my flavor.
I may look down there: those pretty, pretty lights.

---

[1] Cauleen Smith, interdisciplinary filmmaker and Human 3.0
[2] Or: "technology, movement, and reinvention" by way of Tisa Bryant, see "The Syncretic Hinge," Lana Turner No. 11.

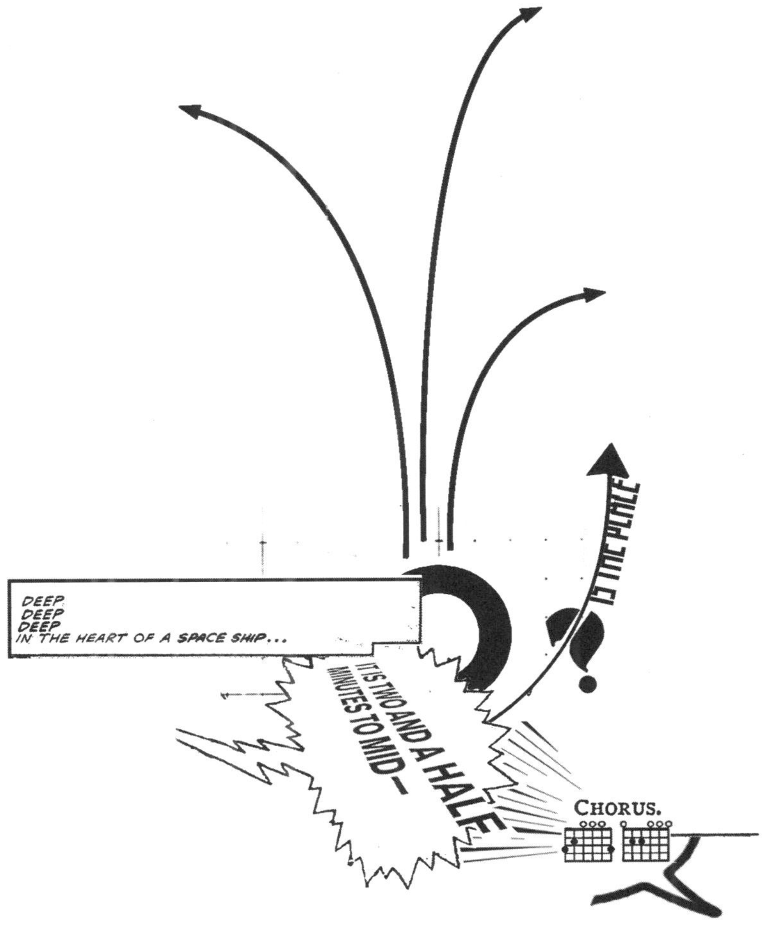
DEEP
DEEP
DEEP
IN THE HEART OF A SPACE SHIP...
IT IS TWO AND A HALF
MINUTES TO MID –
IS THE PEACE
CHORUS.

2nd Semichor.

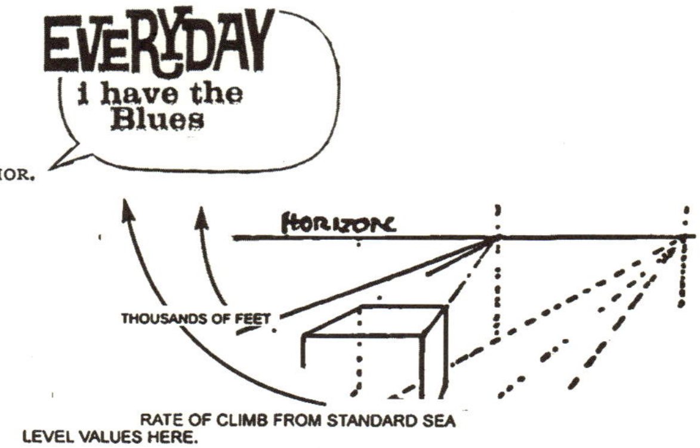

What has happening is.

DARK MATTER

ARMORY FLEX

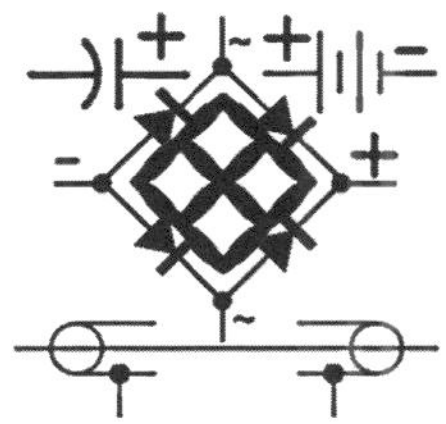

COMPLETELY INTEGRATED DEFENSE SYSTEM

Fig. 1. "Ease My Mind Shell" *Field Holler Helmet*

Fig. 2. "De Trouble Look Out" *Jazz Visor*

Fig. 3. "Noisom(e), Sound" *Dub Mask*

Fig. 4. "Designed for Off the Chain" *Call & Response Gorget*

Fig. 5. "(Hardly) Can Bear" *Soul Pauldron*

Fig. 6. "I I I Strong Stronger Strongest" *Braggadocio Rap Rerebrace*

Fig. 7. "Protects the Joints Yeah Yeah Yeah Yeah" *Crunk Couter*

Fig. 8. "The Wrists Resist This Shit, Too" *G-Funk Vambrace*

Fig. 9. "Clenching Fists Memory Circuits" *Pattin' Juba Gauntlets*

Fig. 10. "But, Black, It Can't" *Beat Tape Cuirass*

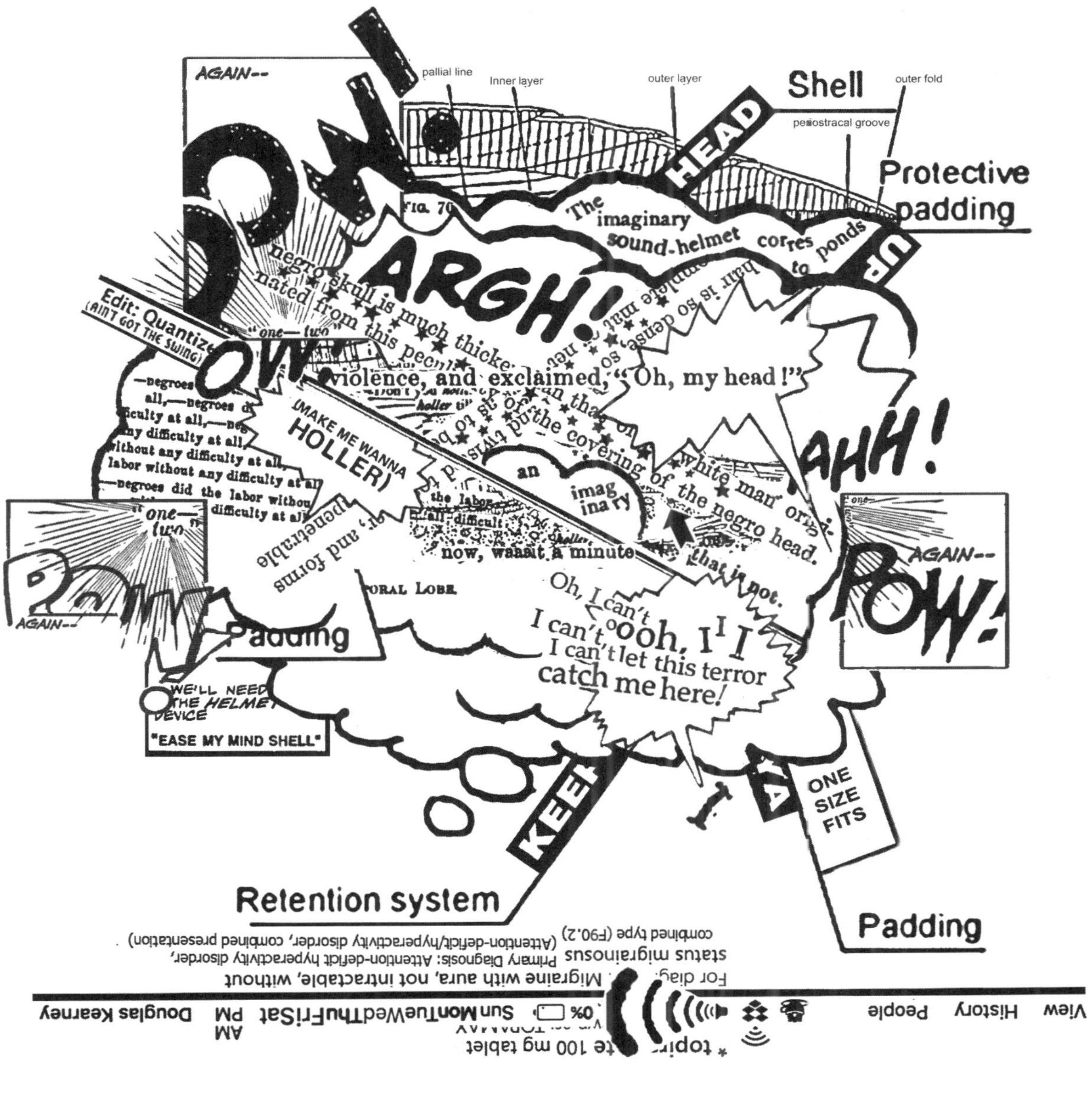

AGAIN--
POW!
pallial line
Inner layer
outer layer
Shell
outer fold
periostracal groove
HEAD
Protective padding
FIG. 70
The imaginary sound-helmet corresponds to
UP
ARGH!
negro skull is much thicker than that of
nated from this peculiarity
hair is so dense that it
violence, and exclaimed, "Oh, my head!"
Edit: Quantize
(AIN'T GOT THE SWING)
"one— two
POW!
—negroes did the labor without any difficulty at all,
(MAKE ME WANNA HOLLER)
holler
the covering of the negro head.
white man originated
an imaginary
AHH!
impenetrable
r, and forms
now, waaait a minute
that is not.
TEMPORAL LOBE
one— two
AGAIN--
POW!
Padding
WE'LL NEED THE HELMET DEVICE
"EASE MY MIND SHELL"
Oh, I can't
I can't ooh, I I I
I can't let this terror catch me here!
KEEP
A
ONE SIZE FITS
Retention system
Padding
For diag... Migraine with aura, not intractable, without status migrainosus
Primary Diagnosis: Attention-deficit hyperactivity disorder, combined type (F90.2)
(Attention-deficit/hyperactivity disorder, combined presentation)
View History People
0% Sun Mon Tue Wed Thu Fri Sat AM PM Douglas Kearney
* topiramate 100 mg tablet

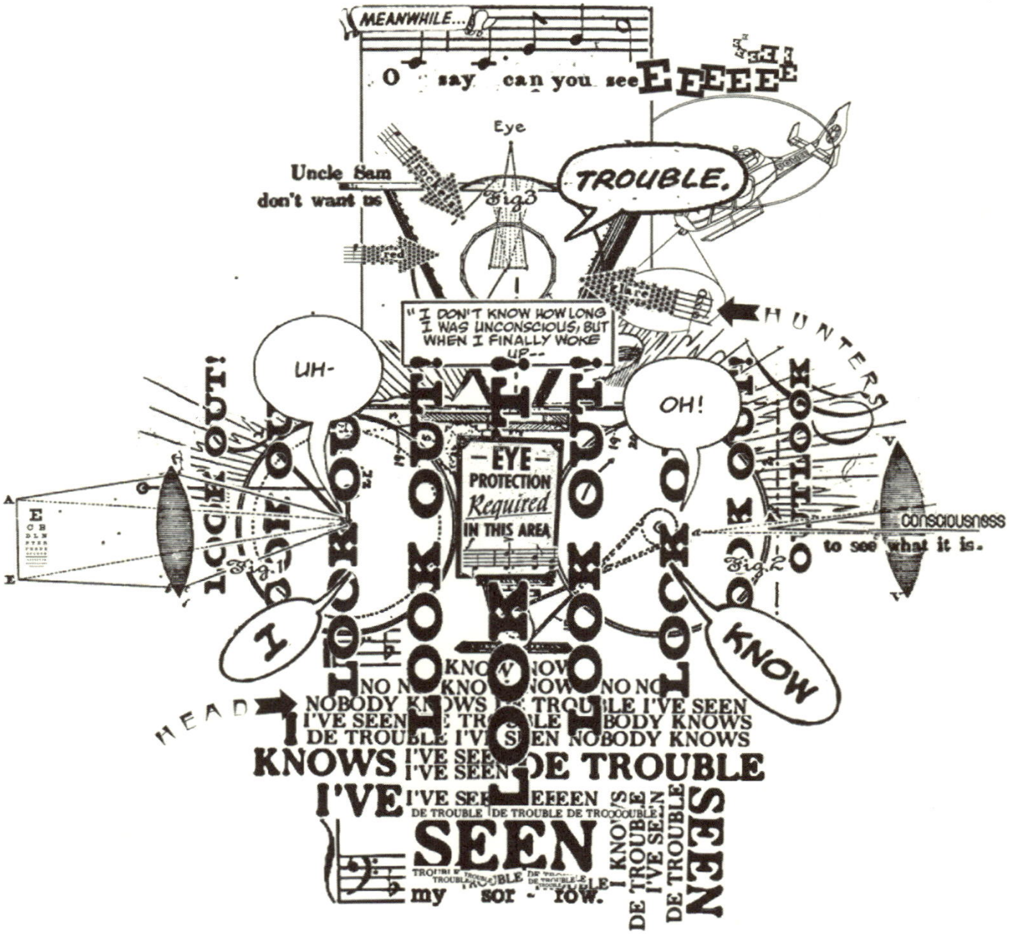

MEANWHILE...
O say can you see EEEEEE
Eye
Uncle Sam don't want us
TROUBLE.
"I DON'T KNOW HOW LONG I WAS UNCONSCIOUS, BUT WHEN I FINALLY WOKE UP--
HUNTERS
UH-
OH!
LOOK OUT!
EYE PROTECTION Required IN THIS AREA
consciousness
to see what it is.
I
KNOW
HEAD
NOBODY KNOWS DE TROUBLE I'VE SEEN
I'VE SEEN DE TROUBLE NOBODY KNOWS
DE TROUBLE I'VE SEEN NOBODY KNOWS
KNOWS
I'VE SEEN
DE TROUBLE
I'VE
SEEN
SEEN
my sor - row.

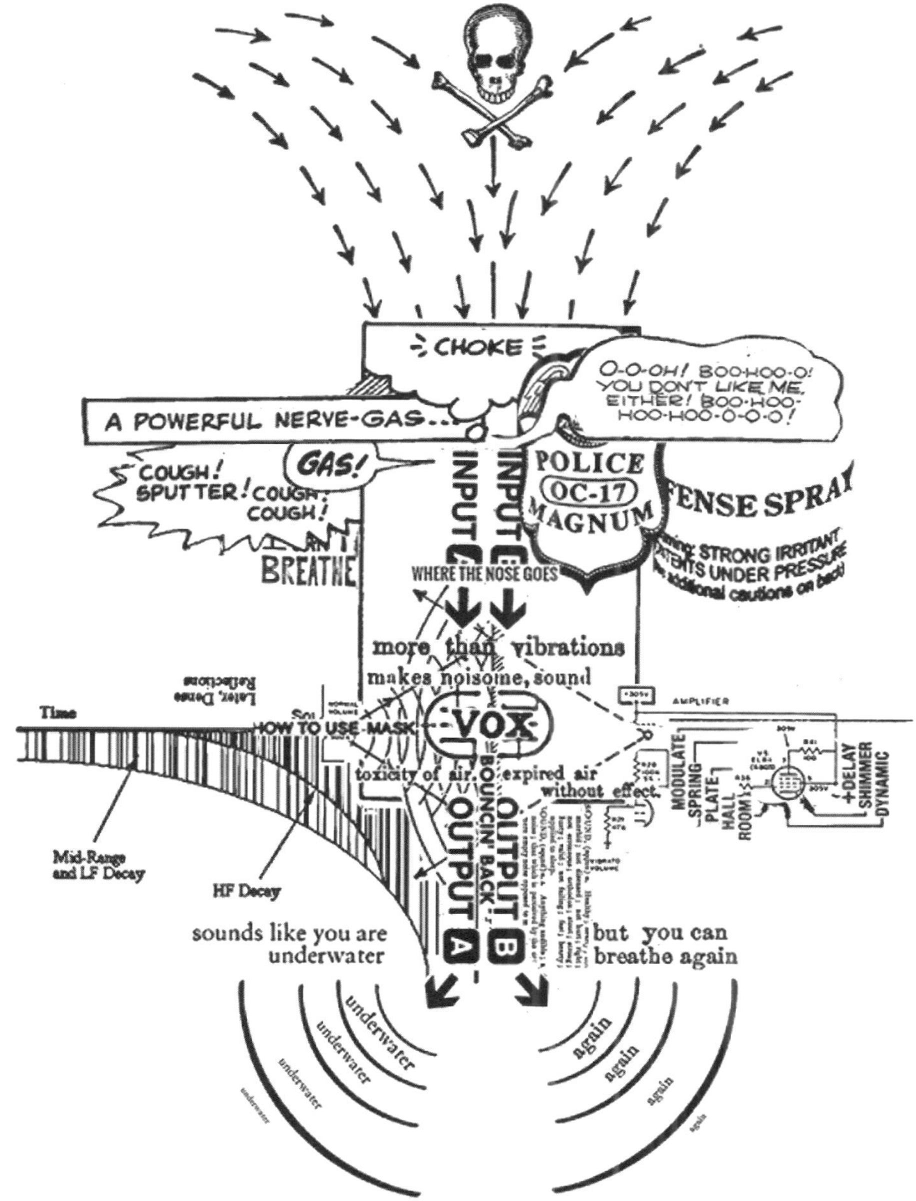

CHOKE
A POWERFUL NERVE-GAS...
O-O-OH! BOO-HOO-O! YOU DON'T LIKE ME, EITHER! BOO-HOO-HOO-HOO-O-O-O!
GAS!
COUGH! SPUTTER! COUGH! COUGH!
BREATHE
INPUT A
INPUT B
POLICE
OC-17
MAGNUM
FENSE SPRAY
STRONG IRRITANT
CONTENTS UNDER PRESSURE
WHERE THE NOSE GOES
more than vibrations
makes noisome, sound
Later, Dense Reflections
Time
HOW TO USE MASK
VOX
AMPLIFIER
MODULATE
SPRING
PLATE
HALL
ROOM
DELAY
SHIMMER
DYNAMIC
toxicity of air.
expired air without effect.
BOUNCIN' BACK
OUTPUT A
OUTPUT B
Mid-Range and LF Decay
HF Decay
sounds like you are underwater
but you can breathe again
underwater
underwater
underwater
underwater
again
again
again
again

WE'LL SUFFOCATE!
3 Three Ways to Safety
1 Cuffee coffles
2 the end of a rope
3 them knees grind
SUDDENLY—!
DO WHAT YOU WILL!
THIS ONE WON'T BE DRIVEN LIKE CATTLE!
0 260667 003459
READY TO COOK
SMOKEY NECK BONES
DESIGNED FOR EXTRA HEAVY DUTY.
PROTECT
Size
Neck circumference
YA NECK 27-31
YA NECK 32-37
YA NECK 38-46
1 off the chain
2 a frayed knot
3 kneecap thee, cop
EVERYTHING'S UNDER CONTROL NOW... WAIT! SOMETHING'S NOT RIGHT...
ked. Cook until center re
BUT, WE WILL TRY!
Cured with: Salt
KEEP REFRIGERATED
Weight
Total Price
27M.$/NGR
9:29
CHEAP!
MADE IN THE
U.S.A.
Best Before
THEY READY TO
I HOPE YOU'RE PREPARED TO PAY FOR THE DAMAGE.
JINX!
I HOPE YOU'RE PREPARED TO PAY FOR THE DAMAGE.
JINX!

The heart shape
Akoma, meaning
"have patience,"
HOURS PASS INTO DAYS...
JUST A LITTLE LONGER! YOU MUST HAVE COURAGE!
struggling
one Stays:
lifting above
pushing above
one Stays lifting
Yet, perhaps,
TIME
HOW TO LIFT CORRECTLY
the lifting a Force
it is enough
it is enough
Ooh,
sho
ortest distance
et
nd
a strait line.
wt = mg / g_c
THE WEIGHT
TROUBLE
g = g_e (1 + β sin² φ + smaller terms)
ATLANTIC
NORTH AMERICA
SOUTH AMERICA
AFRICA
can bear
hardly can bear
self is struggling,
GROOVED SHOULDER
INSIDE...
Actuator
immediate device
for each, enough
for each, enough
THE HARD EST WORK ING
LIVE
GROOVED SHOULDER
ci
gon - na {get be get} eas - i - er.
CONTINUED AFTER NEXT PAGE

Alibi, alkali, alumni, Delphi, demi, Eli, fungi, genii, I, Magi, Malachi, modus operandi, pi, rabbi, semi, Shang-ti, vox populi
APPROVED BY THE COMICS CODE AUTHORITY
"THE STRONGER I AM, THE
MIGHTY THEWS,
FLEX
GUNS, GUNS, GUNS.
OUT
BIG ARM MUSCLES? You'll see and feel your arm BULGE out with super power and energy.
STRONG...
song, folksong, furlong, long, headstrong, Hong Kong, livelo long, mah-jong, oblong, oolong, pong, prolong, prong, singsong, siren's song, so-long, strong, swan song, thong, throng, warsong,
STRONGER...
Annex, apex, biconvex, circumflex, codex, complex, convex, duplex, flex, haruspex, ibex, ilex, index, inflex, multiplex, murex, perplex, pollex, pontifex, reflex, rex, sex, silex, simplex, vertex, vex, vortex
STRONGEST!
POWER A
FLEX
Here's that 2-way stretch new e'er one's talking 'bout re-covered with the beautiful material that bulges Black . . . without Blue.
FLEX
MIGHTY FRAME--

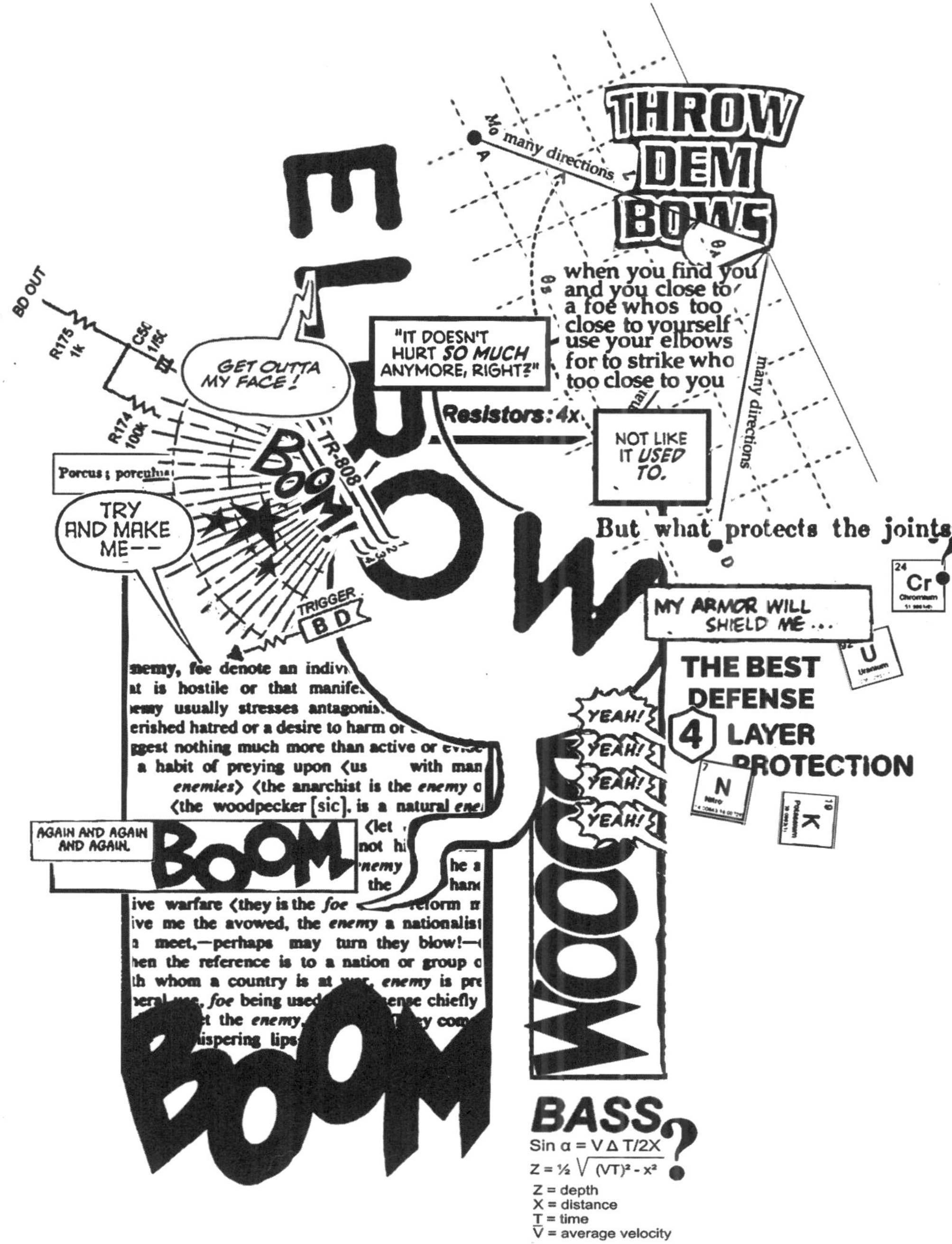
THROW DEM BOWS
many directions
when you find you and you close to a foe whos too close to yourself use your elbows for to strike who too close to you
many directions
ELBOW
BD OUT
R175 1k
R174 100k
GET OUTTA MY FACE!
"IT DOESN'T HURT SO MUCH ANYMORE, RIGHT?"
Resistors: 4x
NOT LIKE IT USED TO.
TR-808
BOOM
Porcus ; porcuhus
TRY AND MAKE ME--
TRIGGER BD
But what protects the joints?
Cr Chromium
MY ARMOR WILL SHIELD ME...
U Uranium
THE BEST DEFENSE
4 LAYER PROTECTION
N Nitro
K Potassium
YEAH!
YEAH!
YEAH!
YEAH!
enemy, foe denote an indiv at is hostile or that manif emy usually stresses antagonis erished hatred or a desire to harm or ggest nothing much more than active or evi a habit of preying upon ‹us with man enemies› ‹the anarchist is the enemy o ‹the woodpecker [sic], is a natural ene ‹let not hi enemy he a the hand ive warfare ‹they is the foe reform m ive me the avowed, the enemy a nationalist meet,—perhaps may turn they blow!— hen the reference is to a nation or group o th whom a country is at war, enemy is pre eral use, foe being used sense chiefly t the enemy y com ispering lips
AGAIN AND AGAIN AND AGAIN.
BOOM
BOOM
WOOOOM
BASS?
Sin α = V Δ T/2X
Z = ½ √ (VT)² - x²
Z = depth
X = distance
T = time
V = average velocity

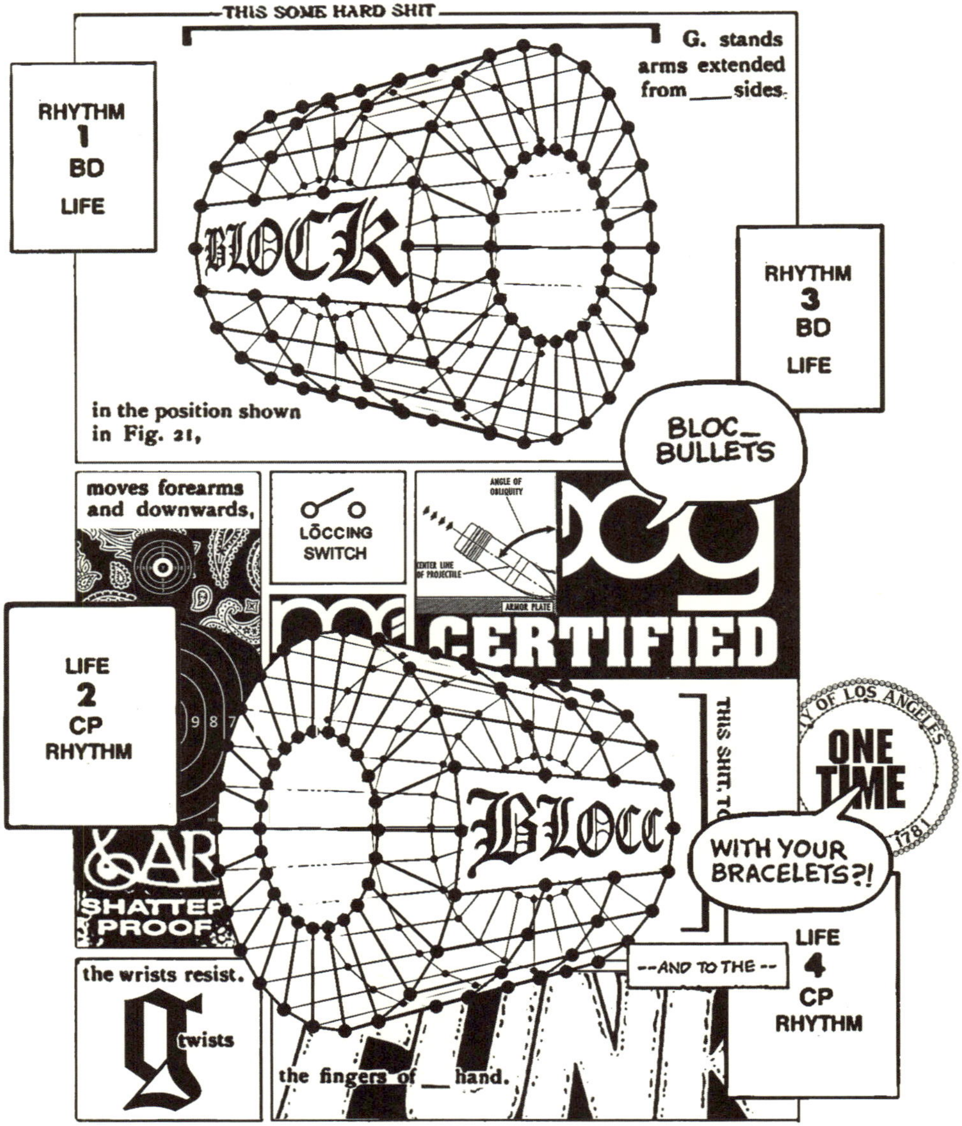
THIS SOME HARD SHIT
G. stands arms extended from ___ sides.
RHYTHM 1 BD LIFE
BLOCK
in the position shown in Fig. 21,
RHYTHM 3 BD LIFE
BLOC_ BULLETS
moves forearms and downwards,
LÕCCING SWITCH
ANGLE OF OBLIQUITY
CENTER LINE OF PROJECTILE
ARMOR PLATE
CERTIFIED
LIFE 2 CP RHYTHM
SHATTER PROOF
BLOCC
ONE TIME
1781
WITH YOUR BRACELETS?!
--AND TO THE--
LIFE 4 CP RHYTHM
the wrists resist.
twists
the fingers of ___ hand.

Fig. 22.

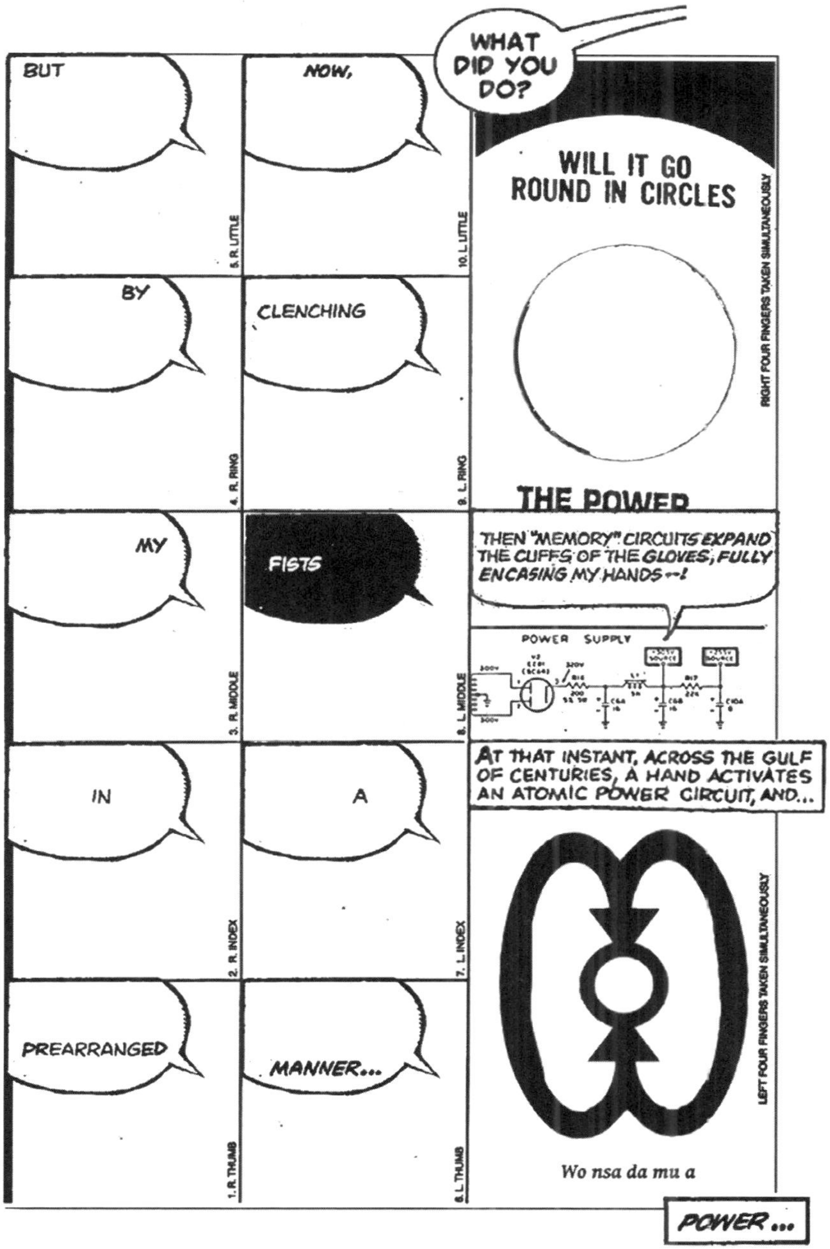
WHAT DID YOU DO?
BUT
NOW,
5. R. LITTLE
10. L. LITTLE
BY
CLENCHING
4. R. RING
9. L. RING
MY
FISTS
3. R. MIDDLE
8. L. MIDDLE
IN
A
2. R. INDEX
7. L. INDEX
PREARRANGED
MANNER...
1. R. THUMB
6. L. THUMB
WILL IT GO ROUND IN CIRCLES
RIGHT FOUR FINGERS TAKEN SIMULTANEOUSLY
THE POWER
THEN "MEMORY" CIRCUITS EXPAND THE CUFFS OF THE GLOVES, FULLY ENCASING MY HANDS--!
POWER SUPPLY
AT THAT INSTANT, ACROSS THE GULF OF CENTURIES, A HAND ACTIVATES AN ATOMIC POWER CIRCUIT, AND...
LEFT FOUR FINGERS TAKEN SIMULTANEOUSLY
Wo nsa da mu a
POWER...

"GOTCHA BACK"
PACK SERIES
STRENGTH AND COMFORT
AND SAFETY

Virtually all hip-hop music is based on a cyclic form.

ONLY

a cuirass loop (No 36) REALLY
PROTECT YA

Really
Really
Really
Really
Really
Real

THE NEXT BEST THING TO *INVULNERABLE*.

?

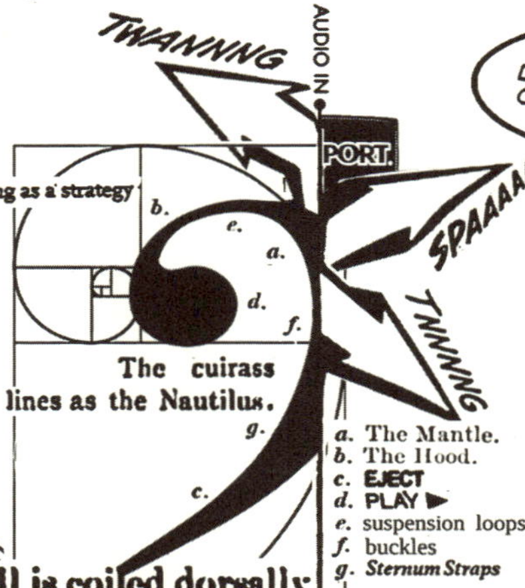

DRAT! THE BULLETS ONLY BOUNCE OFF!

what is it about looping as a strategy

The cuirass follows the same artistic lines as the Nautilus.

a. The Mantle.
b. The Hood.
c. EJECT
d. PLAY ▶
e. suspension loops
f. buckles
g. *Sternum Straps*

1 **The shell is coiled dorsally**
2 **as they run back along the second loop of the**
3 **involution of this loop run parallely, close of the**
4 **loop is a thick, uniting the two portions of the**
5 **second loop of the intervals The two ends of the**
6 **loop lie parallel and close to the loop of the**
7 **beginning of the second loop.**

But, Black, it can't

DRAT!

BOUNCE

AUDIO OUT

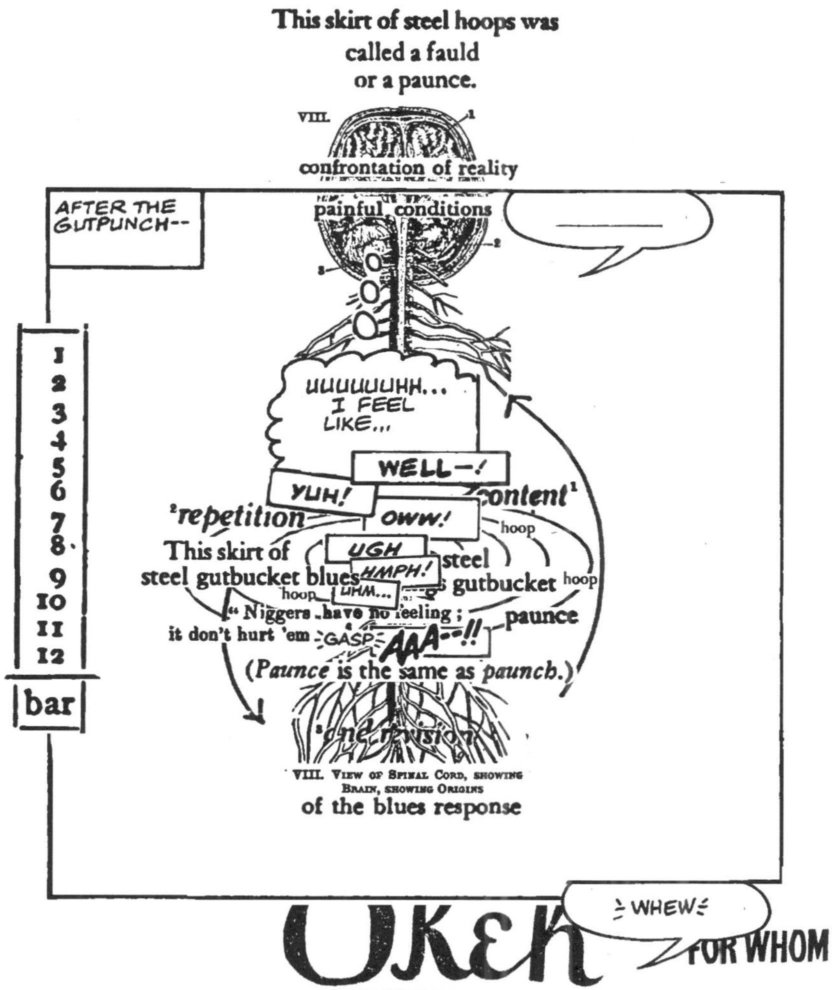
This skirt of steel hoops was
called a fauld
or a paunce.
VIII.
confrontation of reality
painful conditions
AFTER THE GUTPUNCH--
1
2
3
4
5
6
7
8
9
10
11
12
bar
UUUUUUHH...
I FEEL
LIKE...
WELL--!
YUH!
content[1]
[2]repetition
OWW!
hoop
This skirt of
UGH
steel
HMPH!
steel gutbucket blues
gutbucket
hoop
hoop
UHM...
" Niggers have no feeling ;
paunce
it don't hurt 'em
GASP
AAA--!!
(Paunce is the same as paunch.)
VIII. View of Spinal Cord, showing
Brain, showing Origins
of the blues response
WHEW
OKeh
FOR WHOM

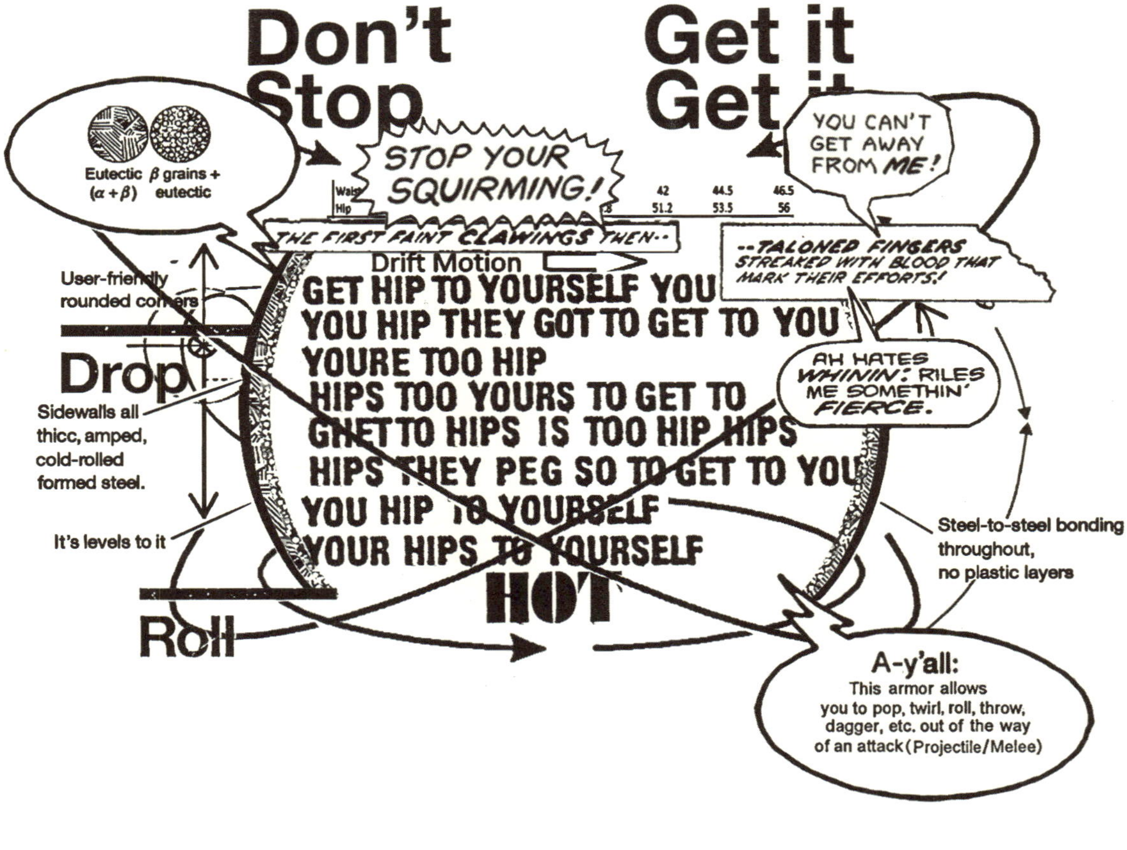

Don't Stop
Get it Get it
Eutectic $(\alpha+\beta)$
β grains + eutectic
STOP YOUR SQUIRMING!
YOU CAN'T GET AWAY FROM ME!
THE FIRST FAINT CLAWINGS THEN--
--TALONED FINGERS STREAKED WITH BLOOD THAT MARK THEIR EFFORTS!
Drift Motion
User-friendly rounded corners
Drop
Sidewalls all thicc, amped, cold-rolled formed steel.
It's levels to it
Roll
GET HIP TO YOURSELF YOU
YOU HIP THEY GOT TO GET TO YOU
YOURE TOO HIP
HIPS TOO YOURS TO GET TO
GHET TO HIPS IS TOO HIP HIPS
HIPS THEY PEG SO TO GET TO YOU
YOU HIP TO YOURSELF
YOUR HIPS TO YOURSELF
HOT
AH HATES WHININ'! RILES ME SOMETHIN' FIERCE.
Steel-to-steel bonding throughout, no plastic layers
A-y'all:
This armor allows you to pop, twirl, roll, throw, dagger, etc. out of the way of an attack (Projectile/Melee)

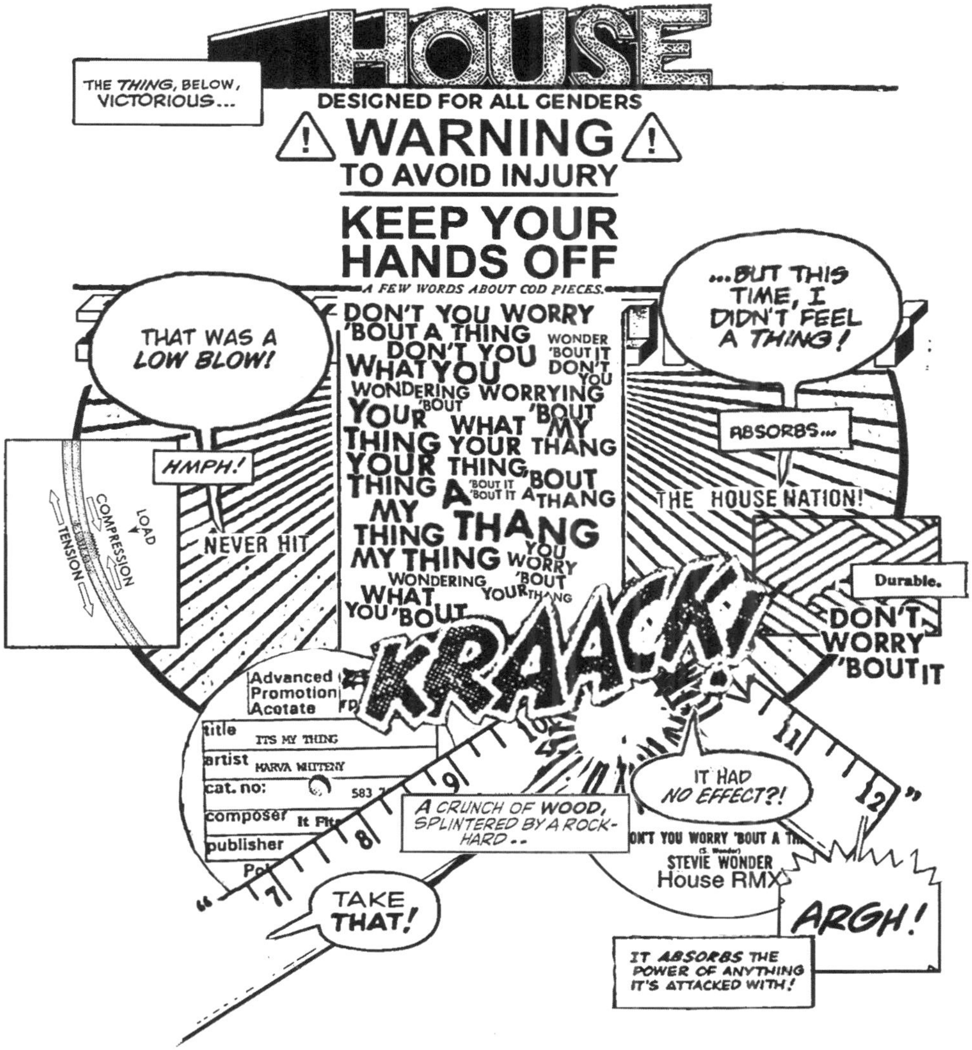
HOUSE
THE THING, BELOW, VICTORIOUS...
DESIGNED FOR ALL GENDERS
WARNING
TO AVOID INJURY
KEEP YOUR HANDS OFF
A FEW WORDS ABOUT COD PIECES.
THAT WAS A LOW BLOW!
HMPH!
NEVER HIT
LOAD
COMPRESSION
TENSION
DON'T YOU WORRY 'BOUT A THING DON'T YOU WONDER 'BOUT IT DON'T YOU WHAT YOU WONDERING WORRYING YOUR 'BOUT 'BOUT WHAT MY THING YOUR THANG YOUR THING 'BOUT THING A 'BOUT IT 'BOUT IT A THANG MY THING THANG MY THING YOU WORRY WONDERING 'BOUT WHAT YOUR THANG YOU 'BOUT
...BUT THIS TIME, I DIDN'T FEEL A THING!
ABSORBS...
THE HOUSE NATION!
Durable.
DON'T WORRY 'BOUT IT
KRAACK!
Advanced Promotion Acetate
title ITS MY THING
artist MARVA WHITENY
cat. no: 583
composer It Fit
publisher
A CRUNCH OF WOOD, SPLINTERED BY A ROCK-HARD..
IT HAD NO EFFECT?!
ON'T YOU WORRY 'BOUT A TH
STEVIE WONDER
House RMX
TAKE THAT!
ARGH!
IT ABSORBS THE POWER OF ANYTHING IT'S ATTACKED WITH!

THIGHS OF STEEL
Figure 1
BRITISH WEST AFRICA
With a 57% increase in coverage and ideal comfort and maneuverability, GAM™ protects arteries and femorals from all type of shrapnel, frag, Mags, 9mms, and colonisers: outer and inner.
Drain-pipe trousers
GET LOOSE
--AN ATTACK!
AND JUSTICE.
WATCH YOUR--
STRAIGHT OUTTA GA
ROCK THE BELLS
--YOUR TONE--
HIT THE ROAD, JACK!
--AN ATTACK!
--AN ATTACK!
BUT THEN...
SALUTE -TO- GHANA
THE STAR AND STRIPES!
THEY'RE FIGHTING EACH OTHER ...
THE BATTLE OF THE AGES
--AN ATTACK!
FREEDOM
dance jams
Hip Angle
Knee Angle
GAM™
Anterior knee-over-toe translation
Ankle Angle
some other movements
IT'S IMPORTANT TO HAVE A PROPER FIT.
BUT THEN...
NATIONS CHEER AFRICA'S GHANA
ACCRA
GHANAIAN ARMOR MODULE
NOT FOR SALE

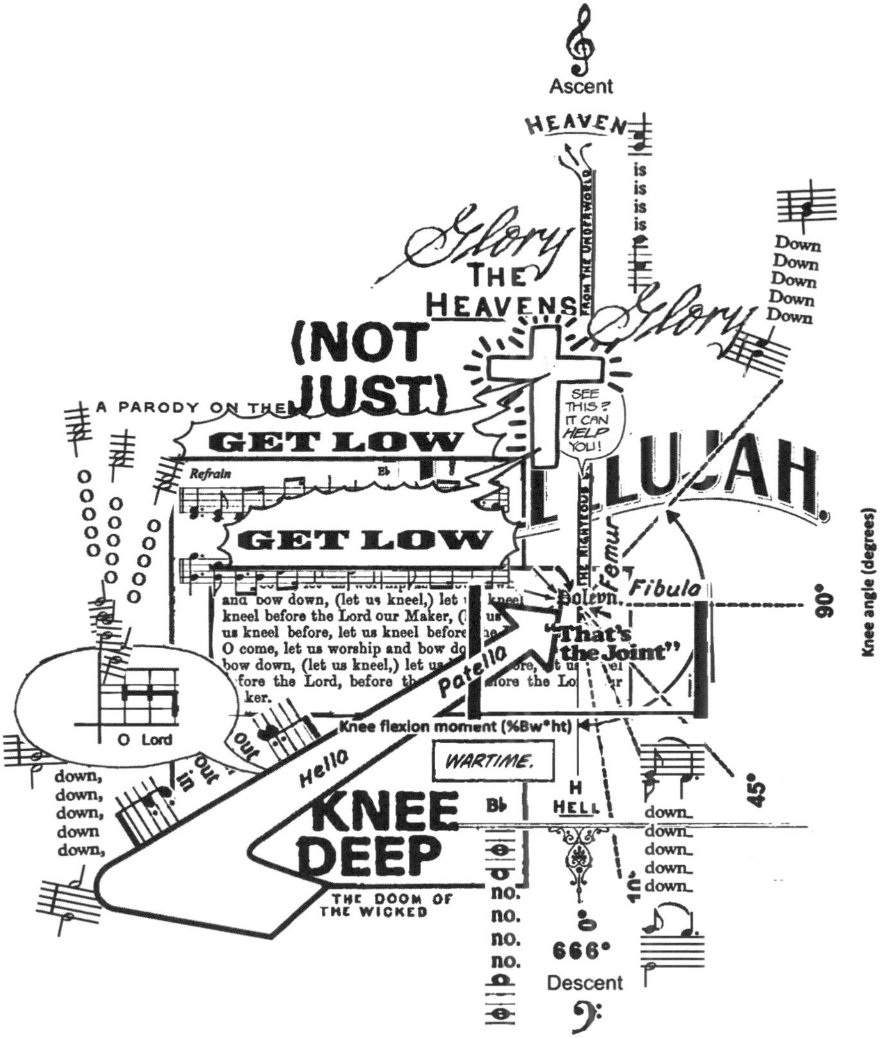
Ascent
HEAVEN
is
is
is
is
Glory
THE
HEAVENS
FROM THE UNDERWORLD
Glory
Down
Down
Down
Down
Down
(NOT
JUST)
A PARODY ON THE
GET LOW
Refrain
GET LOW
SEE THIS? IT CAN HELP YOU!
LUJAH.
THE RIGHTEOUS
Femur
Fibula
Bolevn.
"That's the Joint"
90°
Knee angle (degrees)
and bow down, (let us kneel,) let us kneel
kneel before the Lord our Maker, (let us
us kneel before, let us kneel before
O come, let us worship and bow do
bow down, (let us kneel,) let
fore the Lord, before the Lord the Lo
ker.
Patella
Knee flexion moment (%Bw*ht)
O Lord
out
out
in
Hella
WARTIME.
KNEE
DEEP
THE DOOM OF
THE WICKED
down,
down,
down,
down
down,
Bb
H
HELL
down
down
down
down
down
45°
no.
no.
no.
no.
10°
666°
Descent

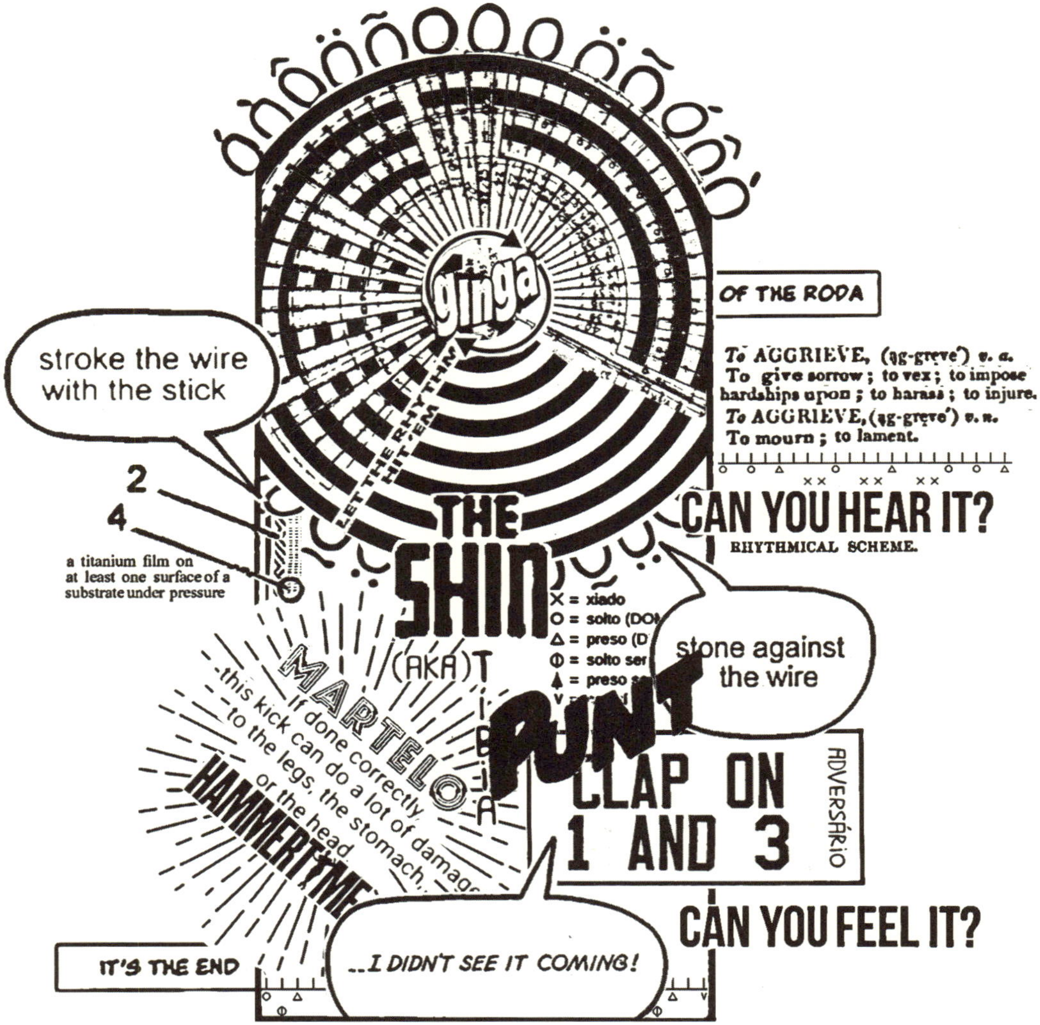

The primary purpose of greaves is to protect the tibia from attack.
The primary purpose of greaves is to protect from attack.
The primary purpose of greaves is to attack.

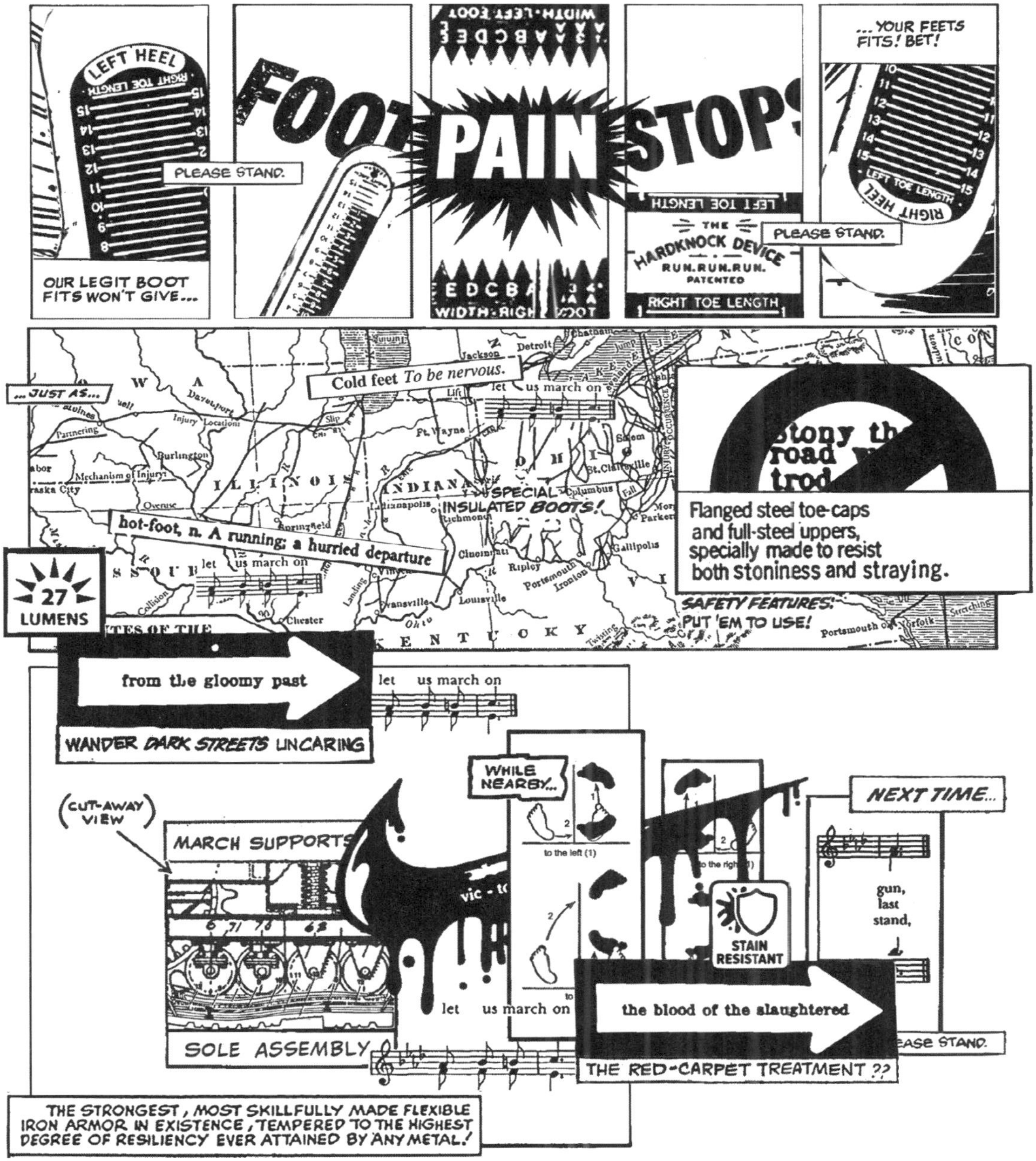

LEFT HEEL
RIGHT TOE LENGTH
PLEASE STAND.
OUR LEGIT BOOT FITS WON'T GIVE...
FOOT
PAIN
STOPS
LEFT TOE LENGTH
THE HARDKNOCK DEVICE
RUN.RUN.RUN.
PATENTED
RIGHT TOE LENGTH
PLEASE STAND.
...YOUR FEETS FITS! BET!
LEFT TOE LENGTH
RIGHT HEEL
...JUST AS...
Cold feet To be nervous.
let us march on
SPECIAL INSULATED BOOTS!
hot-foot, n. A running; a hurried departure
let us march on
27 LUMENS
Flanged steel toe-caps and full-steel uppers, specially made to resist both stoniness and straying.
SAFETY FEATURES: PUT 'EM TO USE!
from the gloomy past
let us march on
WANDER DARK STREETS UNCARING
(CUT-AWAY VIEW)
MARCH SUPPORTS
SOLE ASSEMBLY
WHILE NEARBY...
to the left (1)
vic - to
let us march on
STAIN RESISTANT
NEXT TIME...
gun,
last
stand,
the blood of the slaughtered
THE RED-CARPET TREATMENT ??
THE STRONGEST, MOST SKILLFULLY MADE FLEXIBLE IRON ARMOR IN EXISTENCE, TEMPERED TO THE HIGHEST DEGREE OF RESILIENCY EVER ATTAINED BY ANY METAL!

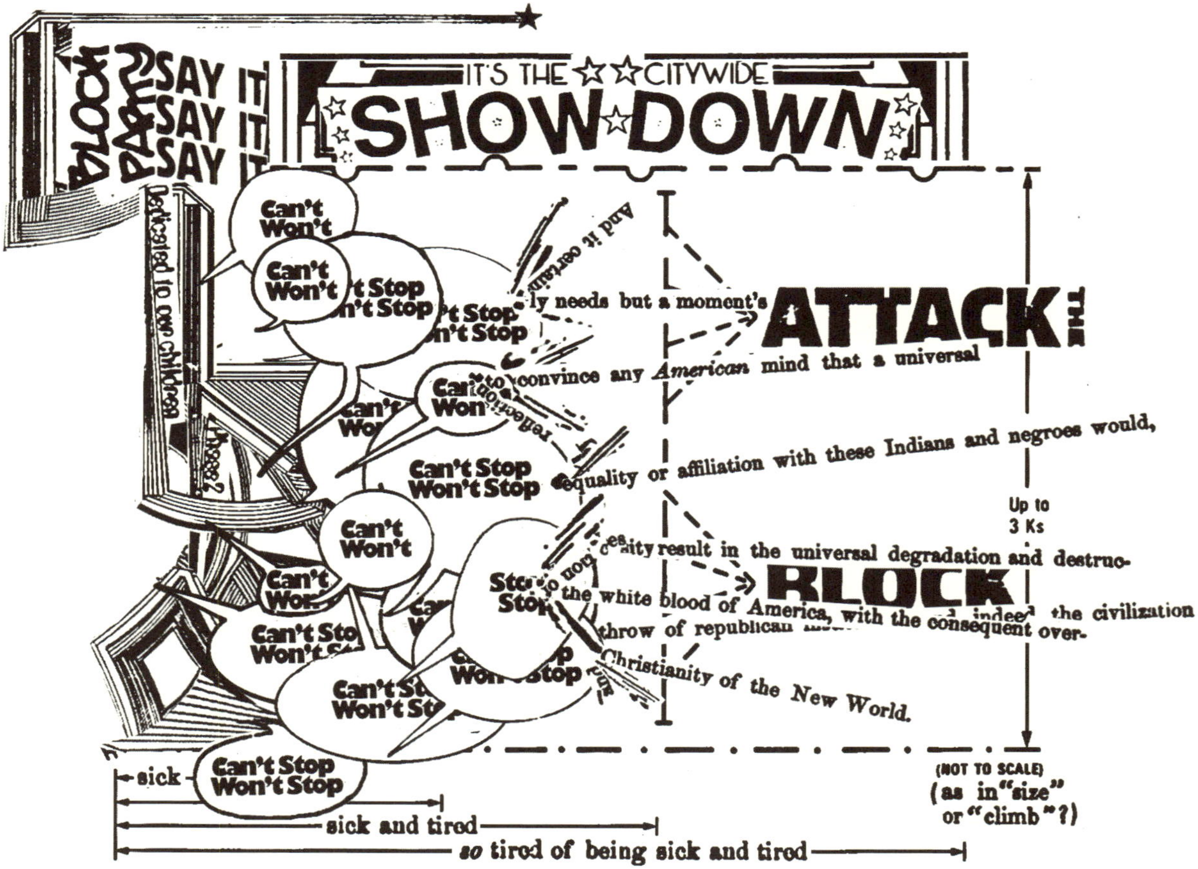

BLOCK PARTY SAY IT SAY IT SAY IT
Dedicated to our children
IT'S THE CITYWIDE
SHOW DOWN
Can't Won't
Can't Stop Won't Stop
And it certainly needs but a moment's reflection to convince any American mind that a universal equality or affiliation with these Indians and negroes would, of necessity result in the universal degradation and destruction of the white blood of America, and indeed the civilization with the consequent overthrow of republican ... Christianity of the New World.
ATTACK THE
BLOCK
Up to 3 Ks
(NOT TO SCALE)
(as in "size" or "climb"?)
sick
sick and tired
so tired of being sick and tired

PLAN AND SECTION
OF
REDOUBT

DEFENSES OF

SOULS OF BLA K

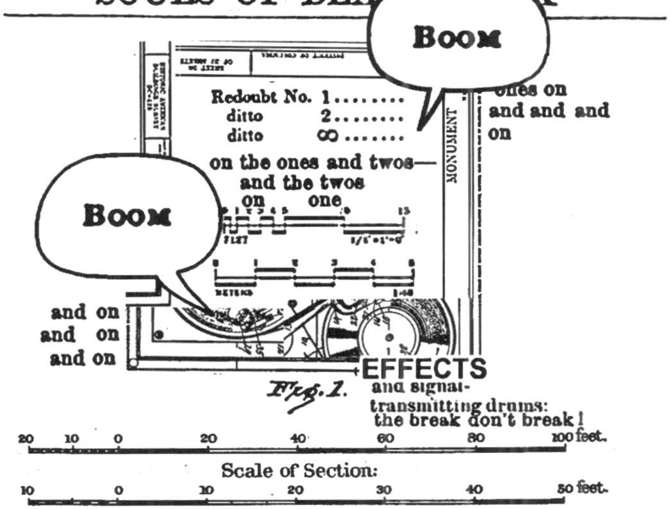

Loop-redoubt has been studied and admired by architects. It would be arranged on the basis of the rhythmical scheme which has been borrowed from.

THAT LOUD-ASSED COLOR

SILENCE: TURNTABLISM

Move the record

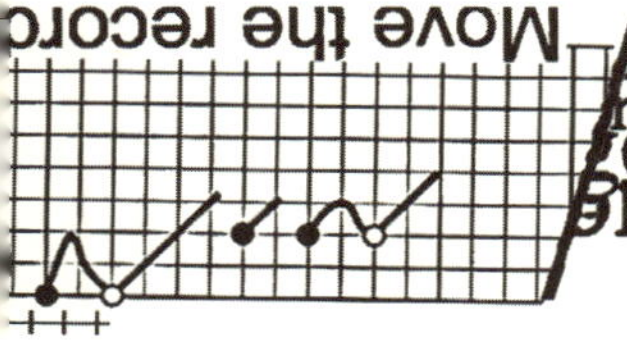

If broken english breaks
nglish then let it be broke.
geometrical structure
of space or space-time

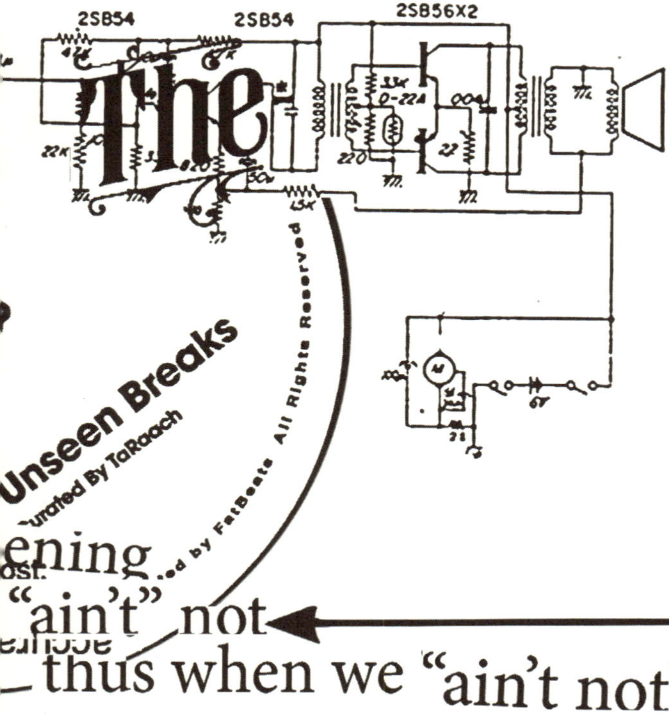

The —break

Drag the platter **backwards**
(counter-clockwise)

THAT

Unseen Breaks
Curated By TaRaach
...ed by FatBeats

ening

“ain't” not

thus when we “ain't not”
we are not not there.
how when one swears

CONNECTION TO SYSTEM

they heard u
Insert quotation marks
they ain't hear

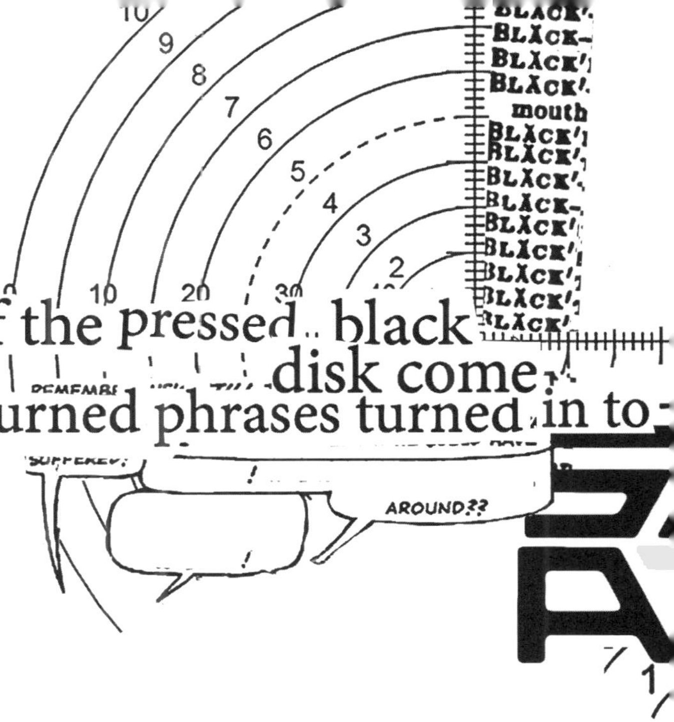

off the pressed black
disk come
turned phrases turned in to

Quieter

newhere
hing.

re
ime

break

ot not there.
swears

Insert quotation marks

they heard us somewhere
they ain't heard nothing.

BLACK–
BLACK'
BLACK'
mouth
BLACK'
BLACK'
BLACK'
BLACK–
BLACK'
BLACK'
BLACK'
BLACK'
BLACK'

off the pressed black
disk come
turned phrases turned in to

SUFFERED?

AROUND??

SCR
ATCH

THAT

Incoming sound

signal *spun* suids in to
what can
4¼ MIN. DIA. LAST SOUND GROOV
3¾ DIA. CONCENTRIC
GROOVE
tur
for a song
sung

CUT

forward, then backward with han

THAT

off the pressed black

disk come

turned phrases turned in to

SCR

ATCH

Incoming

signal spur

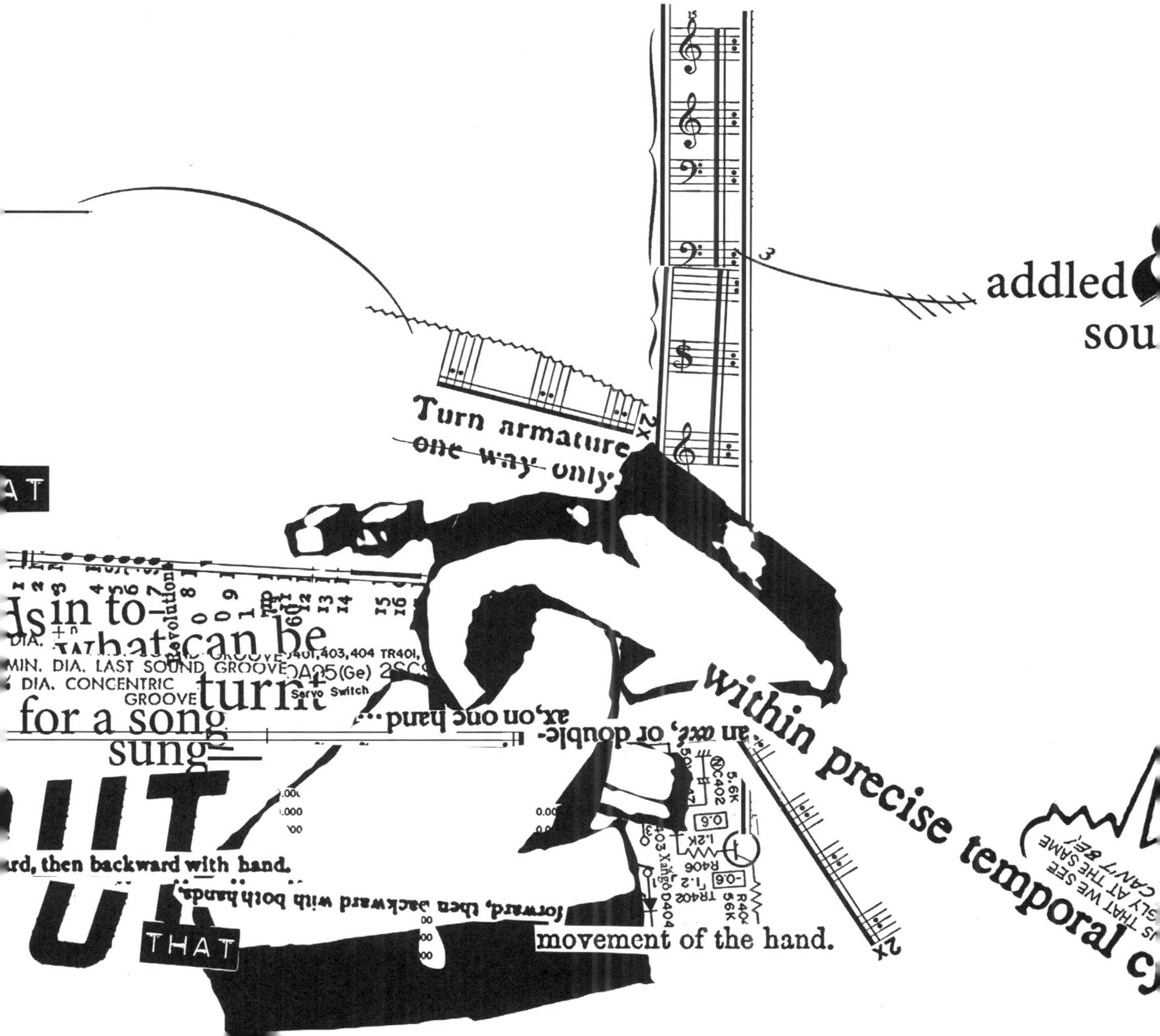

addled
sou
Turn armature
one way only
AT
in to-
what can be
MIN. DIA. LAST SOUND GROOVE
DIA. CONCENTRIC GROOVE
Servo Switch
turnt
for a song
sung
ax, on one hand...
an axe, or double-
within precise temporal
rd, then backward with hand.
forward, then backward with both hands.
THAT
movement of the hand.

BLACK-
BLACK'
BLACK'
mouth
BLACK'
BLACK'
BLACK'
BLACK-
BLACK'
BLACK'
BLACK'
BLACK'
BLACK'

me
ed in to—

SCR
ATCH
THAT

Turn armature
one way only.

Incoming sound

signal *spun* suids in to—
what can be
turnt
for a song
sung—

6¾ DIA.
4¼ MIN. DIA. LAST SOUND GROOVE
3¾ DIA. CONCENTRIC
GROOVE

401,403,404 TR401,
OA95(Ge) 2SC
Servo Switch

ax, on one hand...
or double-

CUT
forward, then backward with hand.
forward, then backward with both hands.
THAT

movement

trying to seem nece
we have known of ma run the
Back'ward, ad. with t
sluggish, unwillingly; towards th
out of curiosity, and the better to a
dull. Bac
you may be damaging your records
the disarrangement of the cur
Backwa
the only remedy (like space and the wire
new ones for which space and plac

time, whereas parole is non-reversible. langue belong

addled & needled
sound dug in 0.000 0.000 -0.0

what the
0.000 0.000 26 25 24 23 22 21 20 0.00

to be dug
from a ro

in precise temporal cycles

BUT THE ACTIONS THAT WE SEE
OCCURRING SEEMINGLY AT THE SAME
TIME OBVIOUSLY CAN'T BE!

and. 2x

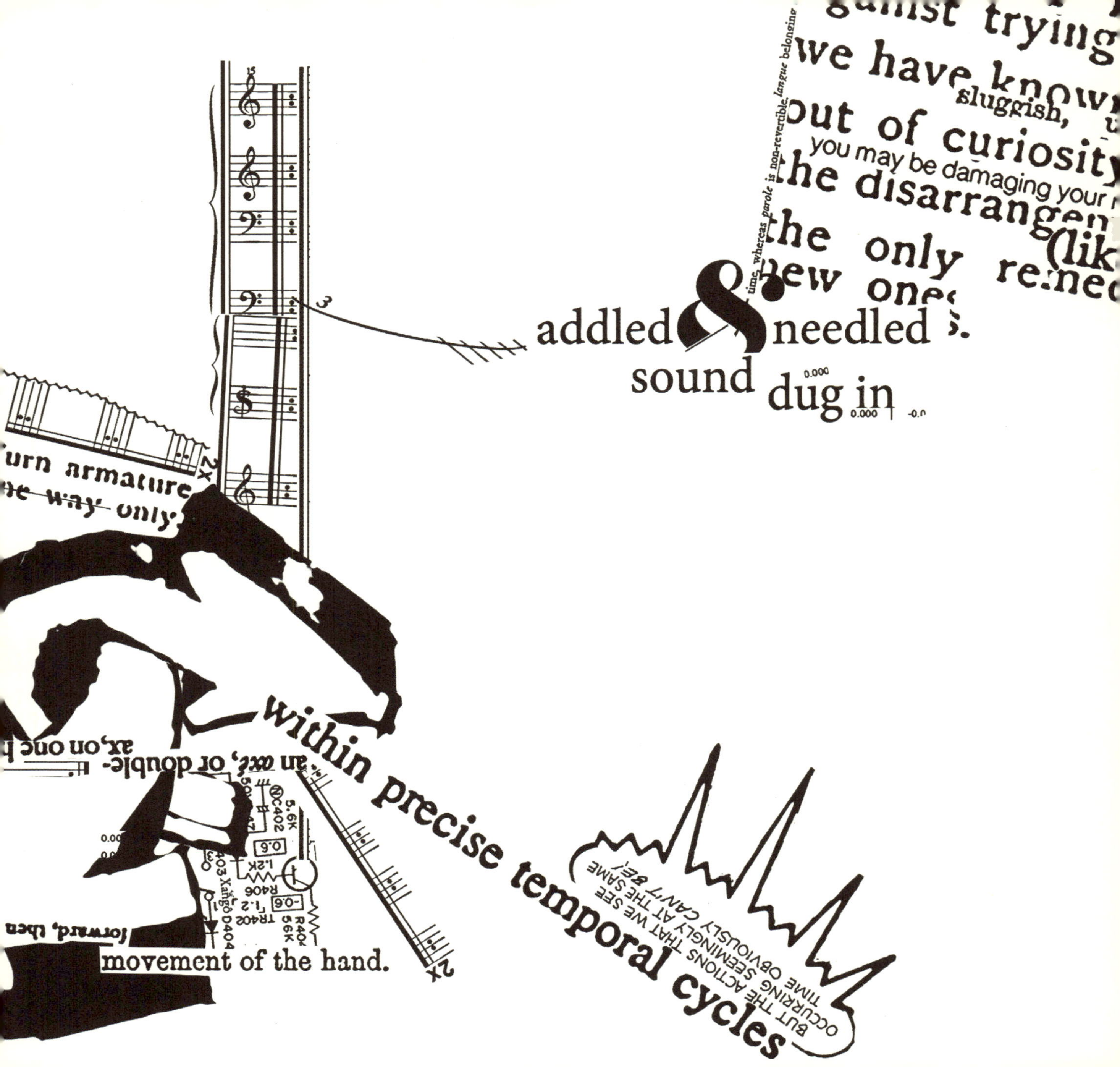
trying
we have know
sluggish,
out of curiosity
you may be damaging your
the disarrangen
the only re:nec
(lik
new ones
time, whereas parole is non-reversible, langue belonging
addled & needled
sound dug in
urn armature
the way only
within precise temporal cycles
ax, on one
an axe, or double-
forward, then
movement of the hand.
BUT THE ACTIONS THAT WE SEE
OCCURRING SEEMINGLY AT THE SAME
TIME OBVIOUSLY CAN'T BE!

seem necessary to caution us

run the armature backward,

ward, ad. with the back forward;

towards the back or the past; from a s

mal better to a worse state; q. not forward.

gly; dull. Back-wardly, ad. unwillingly, sluggishly.

nd the curiosity duly satisfied by a conceptual di

Backwards, ad. with the back forwards.

of the wires in the

betwe

ce and place)

Backward ness, s. unwillingness; tardiness.

brush

or which was the purchase

Notice the position of the label

bell

BMI

what the old masters held to be *imperfect* time

to be dug

from a roundabout black zilch

LOOK OVER YOU

(G. Kerr - L. Ro

From the LP

THE JA

Prod. by rge Ke

Bay-We duction

BELL RECORDS A Division of

SKIP THAT

tou

on some platter the platters must be used to supplement a basic

served on one

The rhythm can begin to move back toward a relentless regu

on one on one—

against trying to run the armature backw
not seem necessary to cautio
we have known of mal
out of curiosity, and the curiosity, duly satis
the disarrangement of the wires in the
the only remedy for which was the purch
new ones

Back'ward, *ad.* with the back forward;
sluggish, unwillingly; towards the back or the past; from
better to a worse state: *a.* not forward
dull. Back-wardly, *ad.* unwillingly
Backwards, *ad.* with the back forwa
Backward ness, *s.* unwillingness

you may be damaging your records
(like space and place)

Notice the position of the l
what the old masters held to be imper

time, whereas *parole* is non-reversible *langue* belonging

& needled
and dug in

to be dug
from a roundabout black zi

on some platt
be used to
served

bell
BMI
by a conceptual difference
between Western historiography
and
African time notions.
45.378
Time: 2:45
LOOK OVER YOUR SHOULDER
(G. Kerr - L. Roberts)
THE O'JAYS
Bell 6 82
THE BIRD
CE CREAM CASTLE (92 51091)
Ⓟ 1984 Warner Bros.
BELL RECORDS A Division of
THAT
touch breaks flow into what's struck
beats at each revo
hands turn songs i
ters must
a basic
ne
thm can begin to move back toward a relentless regularity here
ne on one—
THE TIM
PRODUCED BY MORR
THE STARR ★ COM
FOR SALE

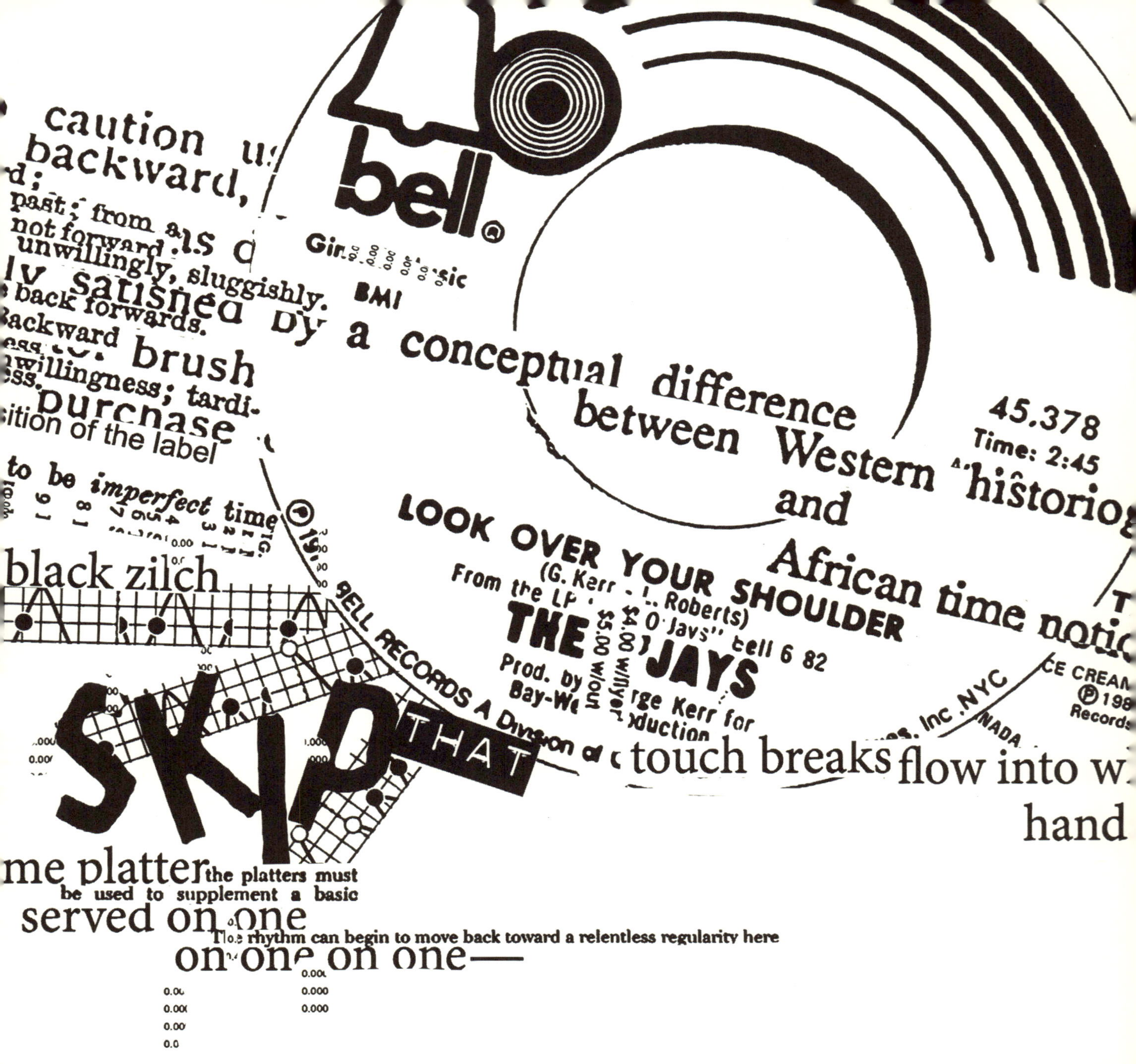

caution
backward,
past; from
not forward
unwillingly, sluggishly.
satisfied by a conceptual difference
back forwards.
Backward
brush
unwillingness; tardi-
purchase
ition of the label
to be imperfect time
black zilch
bell
BMI
between Western historiog
and
African time notio
45.378
Time: 2:45
LOOK OVER YOUR SHOULDER
(G. Kerr - L. Roberts)
From the LP
THE O'JAYS
Bell 6 82
Prod. by
Bay-We
rge Kerr for
oduction
$5.00 w/out
$4.00 w/flyer
BELL RECORDS A Division of
Inc. NYC
CE CREAM
Records
SKIP
THAT
touch breaks
flow into w
hand
me platter
the platters must be used to supplement a basic
served on one
The rhythm can begin to move back toward a relentless regularity here
on one on one on one—

THE TIME
CED BY MORRIS DAY &
ARR ★ COM

turned backward,
in order to move
present into the future.

dj is da time!

In the end, apparently it's just two vinyl
10, 000 watts of
Clean records and stylus are essential to goo
combinations of time and sound, audie

BACK

SALE

COMMUNICATIONS

album
51091)

truck ONT.
t each revolution
songs into clock tock on one on one and
on and on a one-

crossfader is being open
repetition ... repetition, iteration, reiteration, harping
repeat, iterate, reiterate, reproduce, echo, re-cho, drum, harp upon
battologize, hammer, redouble

1996 Kedar E
ment/U

"The
U8P
1 way c

B7 Bm7

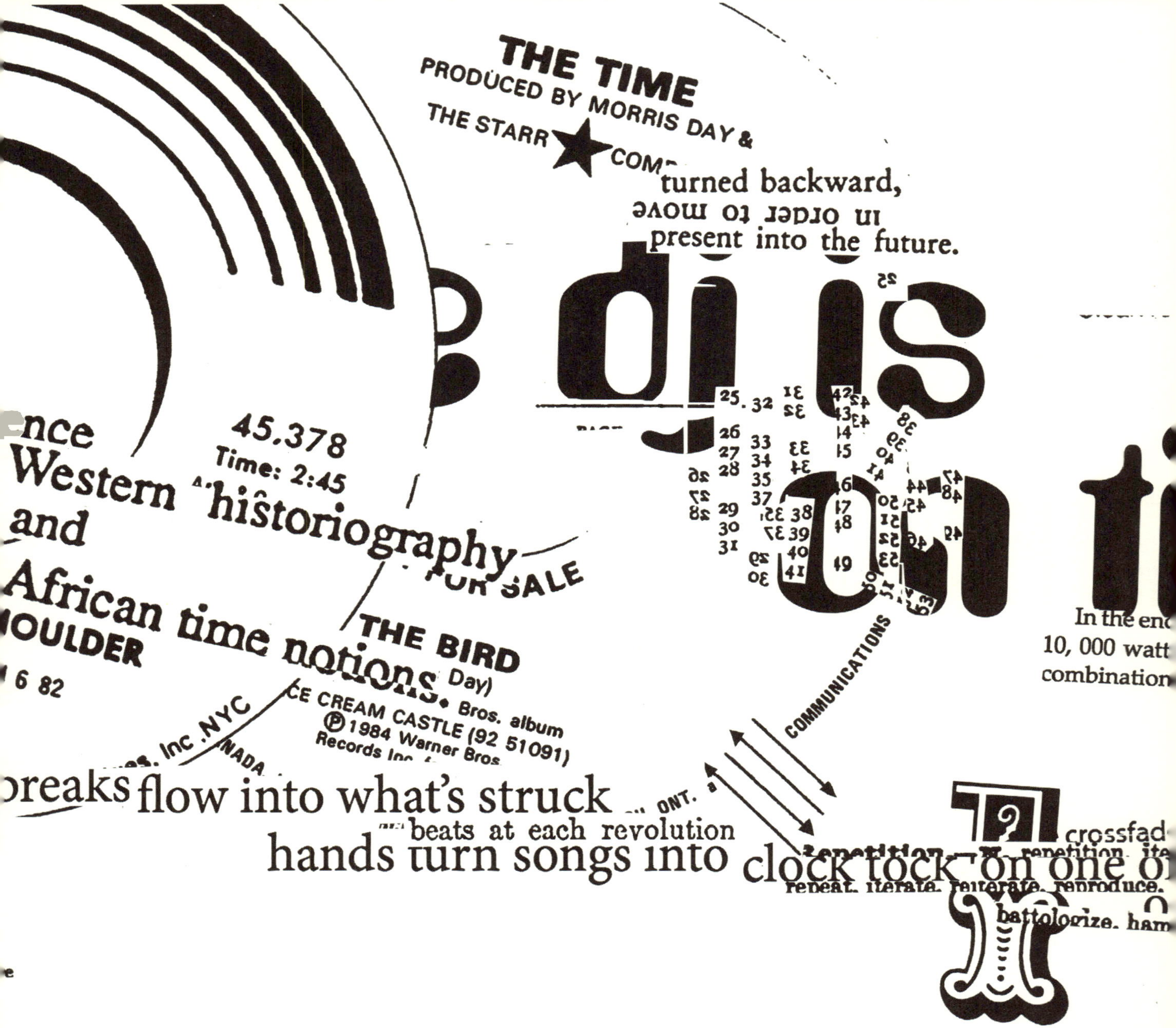

THE TIME
PRODUCED BY MORRIS DAY &
THE STARR ★ COM
turned backward,
in order to move
present into the future.
45.378
Time: 2:45
Western historiography
and
African time notions.
THE BIRD
Day)
Bros. album
CE CREAM CASTLE (92 51091)
℗ 1984 Warner Bros.
Records Inc.
FOR SALE
OULDER
6 82
Inc. NYC
NADA
COMMUNICATIONS
In the end
10, 000 watt
combination
reaks flow into what's struck
beats at each revolution
hands turn songs into
clock tock on one o
crossfad
repetition. repetition. ite
repeat. iterate. reiterate. reproduce.
battologize. ham

Rotate the record **backw**

"noise" isn't signal

ne!

every time you play them

BACK STRONGER THAN BEFORE!

y it's just two vinyl

ecords and stylus are essential to good performance.

d sound, audie

AT 33.3

© 1996 Kedar Entertainment/Universal Records

Printed in the U.S.A.

Erykah Badu

"The Jazzy Soulstress"

open

and

U8P

on a one-

1 way cipher of utterance gone

"On & On"

the thumb acts like a spring the inde

end is formed into a lo

1\.

B7 Bm7

B7 Bm7

Drum Key

Rhythm cue (El.tom)

Hi Hat

Crash

Rotate,

"noise"

time!

BACK STRONGER THAN BEFO

every time you play th

In the end, apparently it's just two viny

10, 000 watts of

Clean records and stylus are essential to good performance.

combinations of time and sound, audie

VERSAL

A

© 1996 Kedar Entertainment / U

Printed in the U.S.A.

Erykah Badu

"The Jazzy Soulstress"

crossfader is being open

one on one and

reproduce. echo. re-cho. drum. harp upo

on and on a one-

U8P

1 way cipher of utterance gone

ologize. hammer. redouble

"On & On"

1.

B7 Bm7

B7 Bm7

Drum

Rhythm cue (El.tom)

Hi Hat

45 RPM

patterns of disruption and renewal

back and forth

(times or beats)

stylus (needle)

when we get our hands on

what was laid down

it turns—"bring that back!"

rd backwards, listening

signal backwards

How do I know?

Outgoing sound

STORY

aha

aha ha ccent, and kind, of the notes contai

cated by the *time signature*, pl

TIME

C (the sign of $\frac{4}{4}$ time)

33.3 RPM

the index

med into a loop

fingers in

J Dilla, Amp F

Rafael Statin, HouseShoe

Side A

til you get to the point

that it keeps on hap

got someones hand in it

Drop below the line

OR / Change a word

no ¶ Remove break

Insert one line space

silence isn't lack

time correction

when we get our hands

it turns—"bring that

Rotate the record **backwards**, listening

"noise" isn't signal backwards

Outgoing sound

every time you play them

aha ha ha

ccent, and kind, of the

cated by the *time* sign

ER THAN BEFORE!

TIME

(the sign of $\frac{4}{4}$ time)

AT 33.3 RPM

the index

end is formed into a loop

the thumb acts like a spring

fingers in rapid

uses three of four

Printed in the

orp.

ss"

got someones

Drop below the lin

tterance gone

Drum Key

Rhythm cue (El.tom)

Hi Hat

Crash

Bm7

45 RPM

tterns of disruption and renewal

Move the record back and forth

(times or beats)

stylus (needle)

id down

back!"

of broken english breaks
nglish then let it be broke.

geometrical structure
of space or space-time

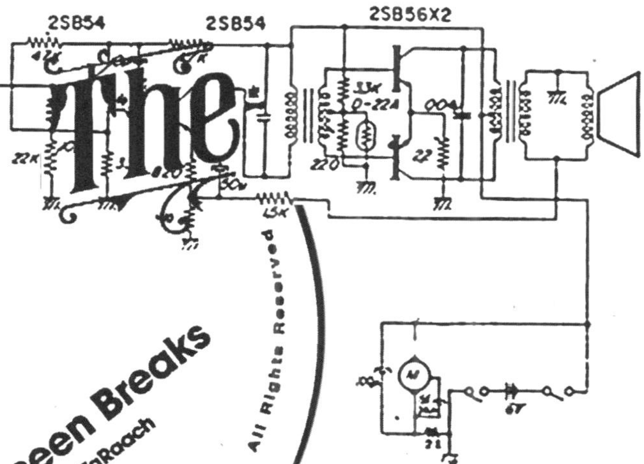

The

—break

Drag the platter backwards
(counter-clockwise)

THAT

J Dilla, Amp Fi
Rafael Statin, HouseShoe

til you get to the point

Side A

e Unseen Breaks
urated By TaRaach

ed by FatBeats All Rights Reserved

it keeps on happening

Insert one line space.

Cost.

silence isn't lack; "ain't" not

accurate time correction

thus when we "ain't not"

we are not not there

how when one swears

CONNECTION TO SYSTEM

45 RPM
patterns of disruption and renewal
Move the record back and forth
If broken
nglish the
geomet
of spac
(times or beats)
stylus (needle)
we get our hands on
what was laid down
ns—"bring that back!"
Outgoing sound
STORY
ha accent, and kind, of the notes contai
cated by the *time signature*,
TIME
e sign of 4/4 time)
2SB54
2SB54
The
J Dilla, Amp Fi
Rafael Statin, HouseShoe
til you get to the point
Side A
e Unseen Breaks
urated By TaRaach
All Rights Reserved
ed by FatBeats
that it keeps on happening
got someones hand in it
Drop below the line
Insert one line space
Change a word
Remove break
silence isn't lack; "ain't" not
accurate time correction
thus when we
how

reaks
e broke.
structure
space-time

—break

Drag the platter **backwards**
(counter-clockwise)

THAT

not"
e are not not there.
n one swears
CONNECTION TO

they heard us somewhere

“ ”
Insert quotation marks

they ain't heard nothing.

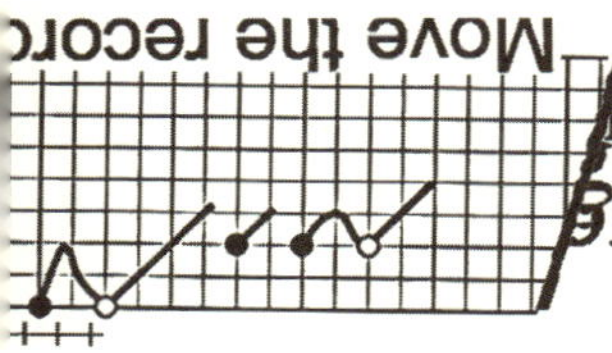

If broken english breaks
nglish then let it be broke.
geometrical structure
of space or space-time

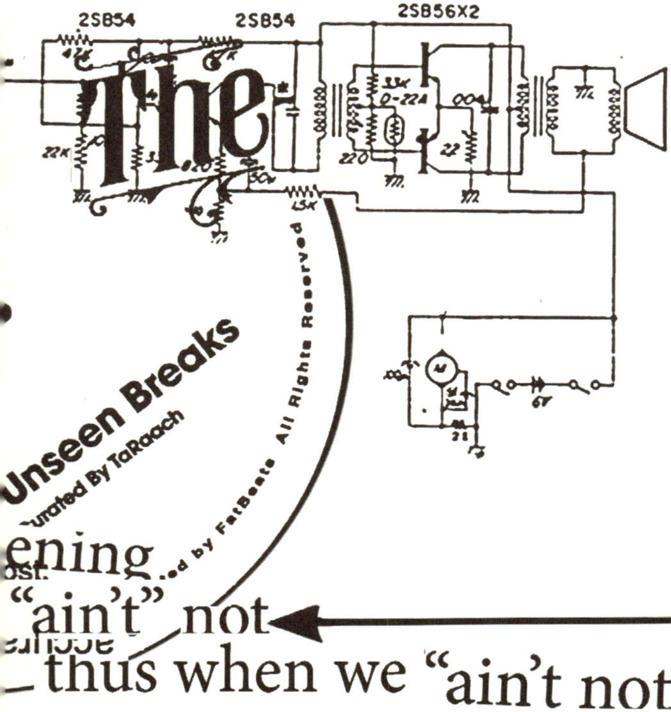

The —break

Drag the platter backwards
(counter-clockwise)

THAT

Unseen Breaks
Curated By TaRaach
...ed by FatBeats All Rights Reserved

ening
ost.
"ain't" not

thus when we "ain't not"
we are not not there.
how when one swears
CONNECTION TO SYSTEM

they heard u
Insert quotation marks
they ain't hear

off the pressed black
disk come
turned phrases turned in to

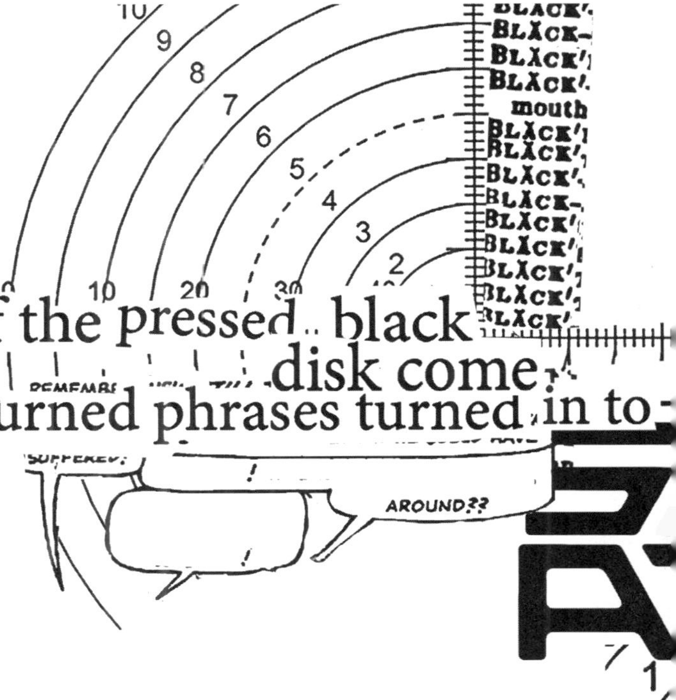

Quieter

ıewhere
hing.

SHADOW, YO(U)

TEEF

What I realize when looking at you I wist there: us is a splitting of certain shadows and in saying splitting what they think of but portioning schisming or headaches at figuring a figure out with our nonstop arithmetic thing. You all *Don't go thinking of them* my bad my same old same old and see I see you yeah y'all said that *Don't* while smiling which eased me so your teeth—by looks too—seem like pills but since you are smiling and I see them all rowed you ain't swallowed them—the pills that're teeth they chime together still that's a figure.

I figure if I could have done anything ere maybe I could have swallowed that other *them* we aren't to think on and left no nothing for y'all to get as ill—when I'd go correctly so before y'all perhaps I wouldn't have spit none of them out even. But now you stopped smiling so have I and y'all all: *For real tho stop thinking bout them*—I'm sorry they take so much of my mind—I'm sorry. I start instead a story of a speculative physics—so it don't begin *Once upon a time* no no no it goes *What has to happen was* and in this story shadow don't see light as what must happen for praxis. At this your lips part some like a smile soon come back only now no no so many of your teeth missing. No

What has to happen was ...

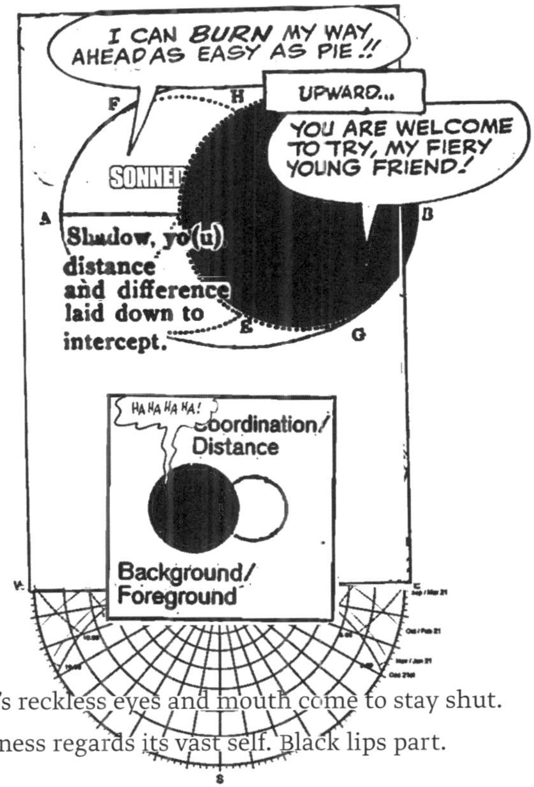

light's reckless eyes and mouth come to stay shut.

Darkness regards its vast self. Black lips part.

afro
PRIMARY COIL
+12V
SECONDARY COIL
WITH DOUBLE HEAD.
VERY WELL THEN, I SHALL DEMONSTRATE THE USES OF THE ELECTRO-WEAVE.
Shadow, yo(u), Shangó axes controller. I mean work. The roots.
YES. I.
Ultra
x
MY UNCONQUERABLE HAIR!

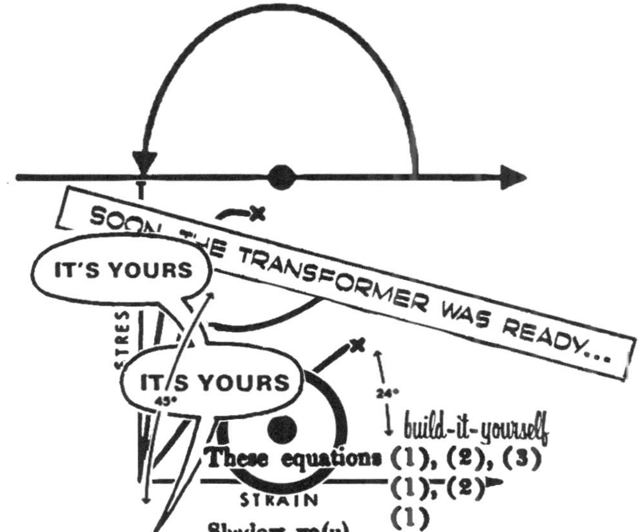

Shadow, yo(u),
on prone
or pulled, gum-limbed,
under none,
you, your sun.

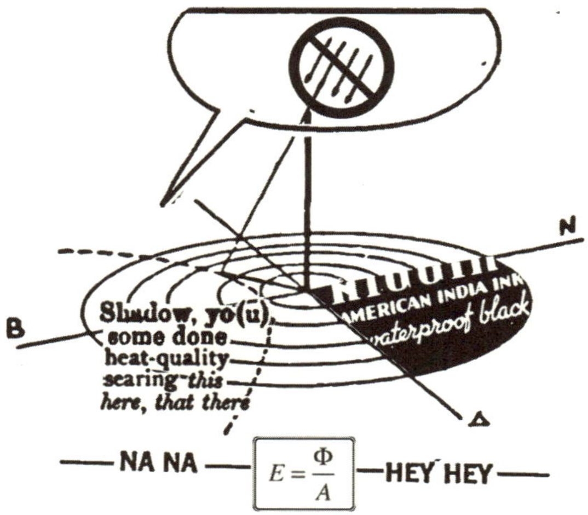

N
B
AMERICAN INDIA INK
waterproof black
Shadow, yo(u)
some done
heat-quality
searing this
here, that there
NA NA
$E = \frac{\Phi}{A}$
HEY HEY

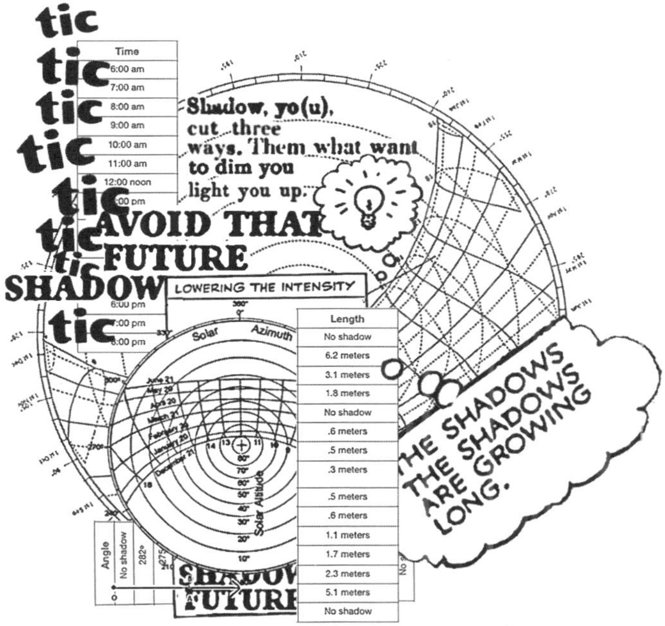
tic
tic
tic
tic
tic
tic
SHADOW
tic
Shadow, yo(u), cut three ways. Them what want to dim you light you up.
AVOID THAT FUTURE
LOWERING THE INTENSITY
THE SHADOWS THE SHADOWS ARE GROWING LONG.
Time
6:00 am
7:00 am
8:00 am
9:00 am
10:00 am
11:00 am
12:00 noon
Length
No shadow
6.2 meters
3.1 meters
1.8 meters
No shadow
.6 meters
.5 meters
.3 meters
.5 meters
.6 meters
1.1 meters
1.7 meters
2.3 meters
5.1 meters
No shadow
Solar Azimuth
Solar Altitude
Angle
No shadow
282°

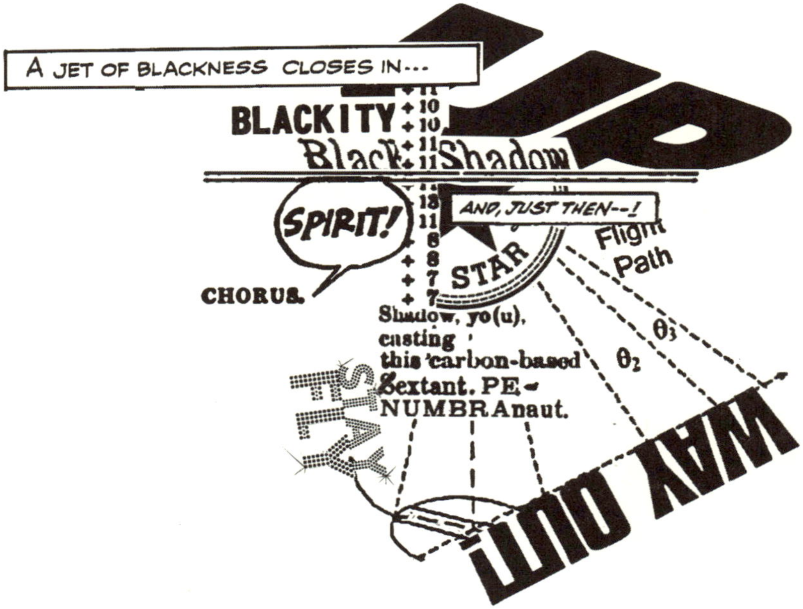

A JET OF BLACKNESS CLOSES IN...
BLACKITY
Black Shadow
SPIRIT!
CHORUS.
AND, JUST THEN--!
STAR
Flight
Path
Shadow, yo(u),
casting
this carbon-based
Sextant. PE-
NUMBRAnaut.
STAY
FLY
WAY OUT!

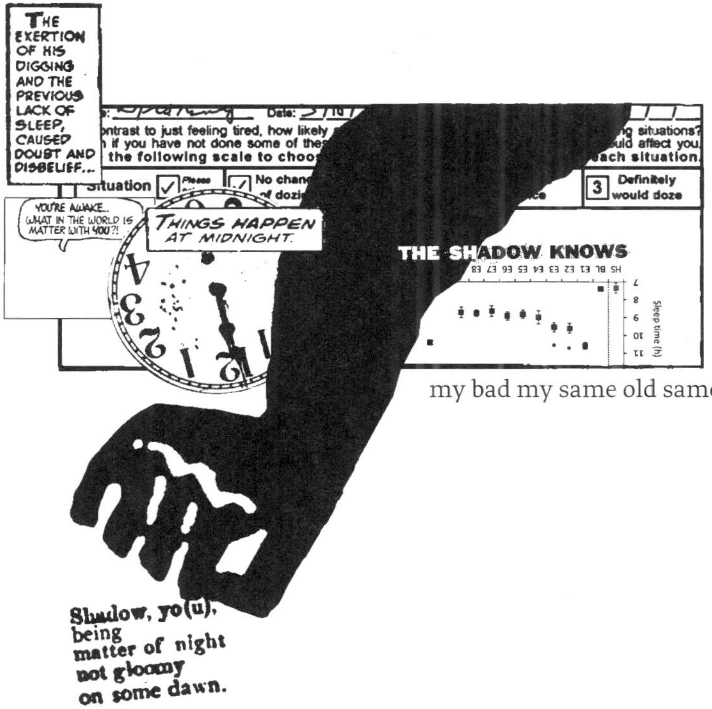

my bad my same old same old

they take so much of my mind—I'm sorry.

UTTER

Existence's condition is darkness
interrupted, by and by dying light—

life wades wide across existence's shade,
rests, there finds no bank. Sinks, fades, knows more dead

exist: light lit out. Flesh remains, bears change,
interred inside a deeper dark or burned,

turned into smoke gone back to join that Black
Range. Bright tantrums, fits, and estranged panic

exude from stars, comets. Some trumpet glint
into gold what's birthed in Earth's pitch-dim fists.

First, what was? And there it is. When all's done,
splinted with nigrescent fire, then down

tens, thousands of days, what raged turns to char;
erupted, soot. Then, some words won't mean shit:

light's reckless eyes and mouth come to stay shut.
Darkness regards its vast self. Black lips part.

WHAT WILL
HAPPEN

ACKNOWLEDGMENTS

I am pleased to acknowledge that the title poem was written using a poetry composition process created by my former student, Teo Rivera-Dundas. It's called a "Robot Voice Poem" and consists of an original poem fed through a randomizing engine for three passes; the original and processed text from each pass are voiced using a text-to-speech program. Special thanks to Aditi Machado for publishing an early iteration.

Thank you to Stacy Skolnik and Montez Press for providing the generous space that demanded *Over Deluxe AF*, a project that opened new possibilities for me.

Thank you to Ariel Yelen of future-feed.net, for giving me space to work out the first two armor pieces from *Dark Matter Armory Flex*; and to Danez Smith and Franny Choi for engaging my discussion of the series on *VS*.

I also thank Jenni Baker and Doug Luman of Container Press, whose 2018 Look Book series occasioned the writing of "That Loud-Assed Colored Silence: Turntablism," a poem I couldn't figure out in time for *Buck Studies*.

"Teef" is written to the younger poets whose work inspires and challenges me. Its ending is a fear that clutches at my mind even as I know it need not come true.

"Utter" owes a debt to Alexis Pauline Gumbs's *M Archive: After the End of the World*.

Many of the poems in this collection were inspired by the work of Romare Bearden, the Bomb Squad, De La Soul, BJ Epton, Susan Howe, J Dilla, KMD, Madlib, Metal Fingers DOOM, Mike Mignola, Robert Rauschenberg, Lorna Simpson, and Chaun Webster. The *Dark Matter Armory Flex* poems were inspired by Rammellzee and Fred Moten's work on love and music. Harryette Mullen inspires everything.

My gratitude to the editors of the anthologies and journals who published parts of this book: *Action, Spectacle*; *The Future of Black: Afrofuturism, Black Comics, and Superhero Poetry*; the *Iowa Review*; *Mizna*; *nY45*; and *Washington Square Review*.

Nicole, about 20 years ago, you casually suggested I was mapping a hip-hop consciousness (mic drop)—thank you for telling me what you saw in a way that I could see it; I love you. E and K: sharing comics, sci-fi, and D&D with you led me back off-planet; thank you. I love you and am so proud of you. Gratitude, Ma, for never batting an eye at Black Geekery.

To my late parents, I hope that in the Up, y'all are still going Out.

Dallas and ChaVon: your ♥ is rocket fuel.

To my grandparents, aunts and uncles, cousins, nephews and nieces, in-laws, I am blessed to call y'all kin.

I am grateful for my friends, even as I cannot list all of you. *I Imagine I Been Science Fiction Always* is the result of many conversations, some held between myself and the people with whom I share every new direction (and many old roads) in my writing life; some with people who have shaped my understanding of design; some whose work has thumbprints, visible and invisible on these poems; and some whose engagement with my work amplifies the possible there there.

Yona H: you been my marvelous traveling companion in poetry and comics since forever, see you in the next issue; Digga: originator of the flash, hope this shit's fly; Amaud J: these aren't cereal boxes, but I'm gaining on 'em; Brizzle: for always tapping in right on time; Evie S: your gentle provocations remain the damn thing; Tisa B: for our 15-year conversation re: Black Imagination and for telling me Cauleen Smith's (!) definition of AfroFuturism; Cauleen S: for that definition and our conversation about MzColeman's teeth; Dr. Finch: your keen side-eye makes me believe I can do anything; Duriel H: thank you and Obsidian for making big room for big play; to all who joined "See What I'm Saying Is: Writing + Image" in Obsidian: 45.2, thank you for tattooing the pages lovely; Saretta M: for plotting and showing up always with such kindness and steel; Dr. Horvath Williams: your formulation of ND poetics (accretion, multiplicity, simultaneity, excess, association) builds whole-ass worlds and spaceships to get to them; giovanni s: for your teleportative glyphic marks; Pam N: high priestess of the Black Speculative, may these resonate with what you have charted at the edge of the Possible; Kate N: metaphor deathmatch and tireless advocacy; Sugi G: for steadiness, insight, and pressure cooker collabos; Jo L: for steering me right every time; Ananya: for process[ion]; Auntie BJ: you taught me to love collage and thank you for your life-changing critique of a comic about a cat detective with a Jheri curl written and illustrated by a middle schooler; Airea D: for telling me where I'm from; Dylan F: for bringing me back to so much I loved; Jo B: for believing in me and mentoring me; torrin g: your observations of comics grammar were keen and clutch; Tarik D: for fearless subversion; Flatline Comics: y'all were my first chance at making my sense of comics present in the world, thank y'all; Kemp P: I'll never stop learning from you; Ornette C: Dō Las visual Dilla isht; Divya V and Joshua L, sister to my mind and archivist to my work; Anthony C and Chaun W: for the retirement plan; Shin P, Monica O, Edwin T, Courtney T, Shayla L, Jose A, Keith W, Diane N your poetry in text and image keeps me lit and lighting out for new territory; Bao P: for the Nerds of Color Death Trading Card series (*Not Gonna Make It*), "THACO" and SCUBA!; Jason Y: for telling me that the Martelo Greaves poem was crystal clear; Khalid B still innovating and working the ink; Shola A: can't wait to talk about these with you; Sean D: thank you for showing me the Massin; Gail S: you've never stopped encouraging me, I cannot express what a gift that is; Steven M: thank you for picking up that issue of *BOMB*, friend, and for your unstinting generosity; Brooke&Brick: the happiest land isn't far away from wherever you're at; to my CC/So-Cal/Twin Cities peoples—thank y'all!; and thanks to Emi K, Demps, and Lauren H for suggesting directly and by example I be messier. For those I've missed, please blame my head, not my heart.

I thank my students, past and present, for being willing to experiment and reflect on what they find. Big gratitude to my colleagues past and present (UMN/More Than a Single Story/CalArts/Antioch/WriterzBlock) and teachers (Noyes, Altadena, Eliot, Muir, HU, WB, CIA) for informing, honing, challenging, and expanding my thinking. And thank you to the staff who everywhere make all things possible.

Thank you to the librarians: you deserve parades, not fuckshit threats.

To the teams at Wave (Charlie! Blyss! Catherine! Heidi! Joshua! Lillie! Matthew!), Crisis, and Blue Flower Arts, thank you for the care with which you steward my work.

Thank you, reader.

And, like when a single, collaged juxtaposition helps a poem find its footing, I thank God.